Managerial Cost Accounting for Hospitals

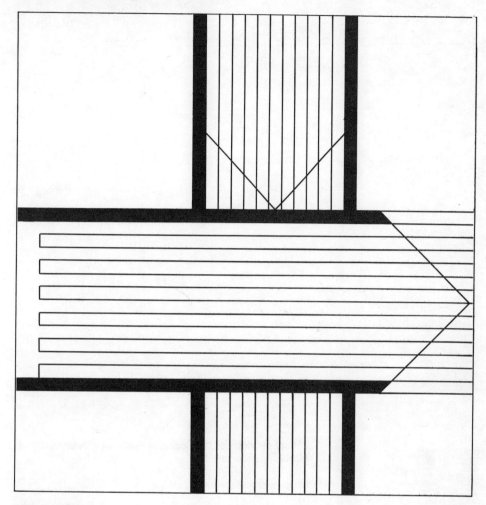

**Financial
Management
Series**

American Hospital Publishing, Inc.,

SM

a wholly owned subsidiary of the American Hospital Association

Library of Congress Cataloging in Publication Data
Main entry under title:

Managerial cost accounting for hospitals.

   Reprint.   Originally published: Chicago: American
Hospital Association, c1980.   (Financial management series)
    "Catalog no. 061125"—T.p. verso.
    Includes index.
     1. Hospitals—Accounting.   2. Cost accounting.
I. American Hospital Publishing, Inc.   II. Series:
Financial management series (American Hospital
Association)
HF5686.H7M28   1984   362.1'1'0681   84-330
ISBN 0-939450-15-1

Catalog no. 061125

Printed in the U.S.A.
6M-2/80-6970
1M-2/84-0007
1.5M-8/84-0051

Contents

List of Figures

List of Tables

Pressure Points

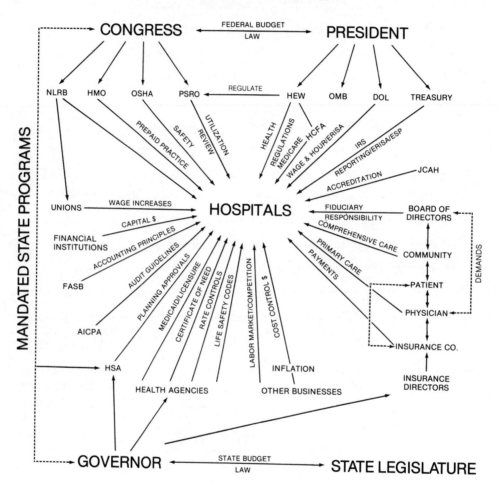

Foreword

Hospitals have already become a major, uniquely complex organization of activities in our society. They have significant levels of expenditures and are frequently the largest employer in their community. Health care represented 8.8 percent of the Gross National Product, and hospital costs accounted for 42.7 percent of all health care costs in 1977. Both of these factors have increased during the period between 1960 and 1978, as shown in the following chart.

HEALTH EXPENDITURES, 1960 THROUGH 1978

Years	National health expenditures ($ billions)	Percent of GNP	Expenditures for health services and supplies ($ billions)	Hospital care expenditures ($ billions)	Hospital care percent of health services and supplies
1978	192.4	9.1	183.0	76.0	41.5
1977	162.6	8.8	153.9	65.6	42.6
1972	86.7	7.8	80.5	32.7	40.6
1967	47.9	6.2	44.3	16.9	38.1
1960	25.8	5.2	24.2	8.5	35.1

Source: U.S. Department of Health, Education, and Welfare.

The health care industry is expected to continue to be one of the major growth industries in this country. As a result, the importance of cost containment in the delivery of health care services is receiving increased recognition. Third-party payers, consumer groups, and federal, state, and local governments are joining providers in their concern for health care costs.

The requirement for further disclosure of costs and other operating statistical data will continue to increase, in response to both internal and external pressures. This will necessitate the continued refinement and improvement of modern management techniques in hospitals. Competition for revenue and the establishment of revenue and expense parameters, regardless of their appropriateness, can only intensify this need.

CHALLENGES — PRESENT AND FUTURE

There are many challenging issues facing health care managers today. The chart on the preceding page presents an accurate picture of the pressures hospitals face at the present time, and there are additional issues that appear to be reasonably imminent in the foreseeable future. Some of the concerns that are likely to be more significant are the following.

Standardization Mandated, standardized, and uniform data reporting requirements will lead to a standardized structuring of information systems. This might not lend itself, however, to more effective management of hospitals. The systems developed might only serve the standardized accountability requirements of outside parties and might not be relevant to effective internal management or other unique requirements for a given hospital. Management will need to address both standardization and its own uniqueness as external reporting requirements and internal management objectives constantly change. As a result, the ability to develop a multipurpose management information system will maximize benefits to hospital management while meeting uniform reporting requirements.

Rate Setting Local, state, and federal officials are expected to continue to move toward cost containment limits through the establishment of the rate-setting process or other budgetary-control mechanisms and price-increase limitations. Hospitals will need to respond to these pressures in a constructive manner and be able to clearly communicate, with appropriate justification, the uniqueness of their individual circumstances. There will be an increasing necessity to measure the prospective and retrospective impact of volume and price changes on various service components and to manage for results. The economic impact of modifying various programs on the hospital's fixed cost base will require constant reevaluation, particularly in light of anticipated reduction in the availability of resources.

Community Planning The hospital is one of the best sources of health planning data in the community and will increasingly be called upon to share this data for community planning purposes. It will be expected to assist in community evaluation of the respective roles of the various providers in health delivery systems.

This will create a major need for improved community planning data and an ability to translate plans into action. Hospitals' management data base should be modified to integrate specific elements of their services into a broad based community plan.

Utilization Review The analysis of services relating to a particular regimen of care or diagnostic alternatives is already developing toward a level of sophistication that will continue to provide standard levels of activity for a specific diagnosis. A hospital's services will be matched against these standards for purposes of evaluating the quality of care and of providing controls against excess utilization of services. The standards employed in utilization review will become a part of the data base for planning and evaluation, using diagnostic groups as a basis for service plans.

Further, the cost/benefit considerations of a standard approach to patient care for a particular type of patient can be applied to optimize intended patient mix in a hospital as well as optimize procedures.

Diagnosis-Related Groups   Closely related to the utilization review process is the concept of reimbursing hospitals on the basis of the average costs per patient treated within a specific diagnosis-related group. In some states, hospital reimbursement rates could be established on the basis of the complexity of cases treated in the institution. Rates could also be developed by establishing the costs of the standard activities determined in the utilization review process for a diagnosis, or some measure of past actual costs could be developed by diagnosis within various institutions, and a trend factor could be applied to develop future rates. If hospitals are reimbursed by diagnosis, there will be greater incentive to utilize cost-saving methods and to attain least-cost quality treatments for patients.

Competition   Free-market competition between, for example, free-standing surgical units and hospitals for patients and practitioners will create increased need for arriving at least-cost, quality services. Lower levels of services requiring less complex availability of hospital resources will be addressed by alternative organizations operating outside the hospital and could impact admission and referral patterns. Hospitals will be asked to participate in per capita or contract care programs. Multihospital systems will continue to develop in the form of combined not-for-profit enterprises and chains of investor-owned organizations. Evaluation of these groups will change the patterns of delivery of health care services.

   The economics of these activities, the impact on the competing free-standing community hospitals and on the alternative providers, require a sophisticated level of financial analysis. Increased usage of contract services, such as housekeeping, cafeteria, and electronic data processing, will also require the understanding and use of financial and statistical information for proper decision making.

MECHANISM FOR RESPONSE

The American Hospital Association's Council on Finance in March 1977 established a Special Committee on Financial Publications and charged it to review and update the 1968 AHA publication, *Cost Finding and Rate Setting.* The committee concluded that cost finding was no longer adequate to meet the cost information needs of health care institutions and was, in fact, contributing to inequities in the payment systems of various payers. The committee further recognized that the complexity and range of services in health care delivery vary significantly from one hospital to another and a uniform, rigid set of rules for all hospitals is not viable. Instead, there is a real need for common principles and application criteria that can be tailored to individual situations.

   In light of both present and future challenges facing hospitals, the inadequacy of cost finding, and the uniqueness of individual hospitals, the committee developed this publication. It is intended to bring modern cost accounting techniques to hospitals and provide health care managers with a mechanism for improved response to present and future issues in health care delivery.

The members of the American Hospital Association Special Committee for Financial Publications responsible for the development of this manual were Chairman Joseph P. McCue, director of fiscal affairs, Massachusetts General Hospital, Boston; Raymond J. Cisneros, vice-president/financial operations, Affiliated Hospital Center, Inc., Boston; Crawford R. Hardy, vice-president and treasurer, Pacific Health Resources, Los Angeles; Merton H. Walters, vice-president/finance, Greater Cleveland (OH) Hospital Association; John E. Wendling, partner, Elmer Fox, Westheimer & Company, Topeka, KS; and secretary, Isaac C. Mensah, AHA Division of Financial Management, Chicago.

Kelly F. Guncheon, assistant editor, and Dorothy Saxner, manager, AHA Books and Newsletters, provided editing services.

W. Glenn Cannon, partner, Los Angeles, and G. Byron Thompson, director of health care consulting services, Chicago, both of Coopers & Lybrand, served as consultants and wrote the publication at the committee's direction.

SECTION I. FUNDAMENTALS OF COST ACCOUNTING

Chapter 1. INTRODUCTION
Chapter 2. COST CLASSIFICATION AND BEHAVIOR

CHAPTER **1**

Introduction

Today's hospital is a highly complex organization of multiple resources. In the face of rising costs, growing external regulatory requirements, and rapidly changing health care technology, administration of the hospital requires the application of the most sophisticated management techniques.

During the 1970s, many hospital financial managers have relied on cost-finding techniques both to satisfy the hospital's internal financial information needs and to meet the external cost reporting requirements of third-party payers (Medicare, Medicaid, and other governmental and privately financed programs). Most managers recognize certain shortcomings of cost-finding techniques, and many have struggled to develop new ways of applying less arbitrary methods of cost determination.

In order to respond to the need for improvement of current financial systems in hospitals, the American Hospital Association commissioned the Special Committee on Financial Publications of the AHA Council on Finance to develop a publication that details innovative cost accounting techniques for hospitals. This manual has been prepared to offer hospitals of any size more sophisticated methodologies for making accurate and timely determinations of the costs required to provide all services. The principles of cost accounting that have been established in other industries for many years and that have been generally applied by the accounting profession are here extended to hospitals. This publication is intended to provide a clear understanding of the concepts involved in and a practical means of implementing cost planning and measurement principles and applications in hospitals.

The objectives of a viable system of cost accounting in a hospital should include:

- A common basis for communication, negotiation, planning, and management for all levels of hospital personnel and also between hospitals and regulators.
- A method of measuring the effects of changes in intensity and case mix.
- A method of evaluating and measuring performance against a plan.
- A way to provide managers of all levels with the information required to manage resources efficiently. Standards developed in this process allow managers to forecast labor and nonlabor expenses based on levels of utilization over short intervals.
- A method to assist management in identifying those costs that can be converted from fixed to variable. If the method is undertaken, downturns in volume will be less critical to the financial well-being of the hospital.
- A method of identifying inefficient functions and demonstrating the nature of the problem, such as price, volume, or practice.

A hospital cost accounting system should include two elements: a basic cost information system and a cost accounting system. These two elements relate directly to the two basic segments in this work.

BASIC COST INFORMATION SYSTEM

This text first presents a basic cost information system, which is detailed in section II. This system accounts for costs by responsibility center and generates basic management performance reports. The planning and measuring of costs and output by activity center or functional grouping offers the data foundation for cost management. It also provides an articulation of costs and performance against the budget plan under various configurations of reporting.

 To implement this system, several steps are necessary:

- Accumulating, accounting for, and assigning costs after they are initially identified with an individual department or cost center to a patient care department
- Carefully measuring the volume of output of each cost center or function
- Utilizing various cost analysis techniques in determining the financial appropriateness of certain operating or capital decisions.

COST ACCOUNTING SYSTEM

The basic cost information system, although an improvement over cost finding, does not provide management with sufficient information to do flexible budgeting or variance analysis. Section III, on the cost accounting system, details the system enhancements that need to be in place to carry out these important functions.

The principal elements of a cost accounting system include:

- Identifying activities by which performance will be measured
- Establishing standards for each activity to be measured
- Maintaining the system to update standards

- Collecting detailed statistical and financial information
- Displaying data that enable managers to look at costs and statistics by patient, cost or revenue sharing, and diagnosis groupings
- A timely and accurate flexible budgeting system with performance reports that include variances for each department, function, or cost center

It should be noted that standards include labor, materials, volume, or other types of standards that can be compared with actual results for the purposes of measuring performance. The predetermination of various standards permits management to carefully examine its operations and isolate those individual factors that can contribute to cost changes.

This system is the heart of the hospital information system. The information provided is equally useful for:

- Long-range planning
- Financial analysis with respect to expanding or contracting specific services
- Evaluating performance of departmental staff and management
- Budget review and rate setting
- Satisfying external reporting requirements

The cost accounting system described in this text is a system that will move hospitals closer to the development of patient-by-patient cost determination while simultaneously providing for performance measurement on the existing departmental or cost center basis.

APPLICABILITY OF MANAGERIAL COST ACCOUNTING

The managerial cost accounting system presented in this text is based on a practical application under existing circumstances. As will be seen, it is a hybrid system combining features of both process and job order cost systems. It provides a viable mechanism for response to the challenging issues facing hospital managers, and can meet the management requirements that presently exist and can be anticipated in the forseeable future, whether initiated internally or externally.

Ideally, a pure job order cost accounting system appears the most desirable for a hospital's operations. It would allow each specific cost to be clearly identified with the appropriate patient on the basis of diagnosis category and provide for a patient-by-patient cost identification system. Of course, at the present time such a system would be highly ambitious for even the most sophisticated hospital. However, it is not outside the realm of future possibility.

In any event, the hybrid system delineated in this text can deliver measurable benefit in three important ways. It can:

- Provide a means for meeting managerial requirements and significantly improve existing management systems
- Provide reasonably comfortable assurance that the increasingly dynamic and changing pressures on hospitals can be dealt with efficiently and effectively with minimal sacrifice to the health care delivery system
- Provide a major step in beginning the establishment of a data base that will allow improvement in the system of managing and delivering future health care services

DATA BASE MANAGEMENT SYSTEMS

Hospitals will be required to provide additional financial and statistical information that is readily usable for management and modified, if necessary, for reporting and accountability purposes. This requirement calls for a flexible data base. To develop and maintain a flexible data base is an expensive undertaking. However, the magnitude of total economic resources controlled by a hospital today is significant, and there is an increasing availability of data processing systems to serve other hospital functions that can yield necessary information for a data base. The cost/benefit relationship for data base systems is improving.

Hospitals continue to experience an increasing number of automated data processing applications for fundamental patient care activities. These activities include admission, discharge and transfer of patients, patient mix determination, laboratory services, nurse-staffing and scheduling applications, pharmacy, and basic support systems such as the accounting function for labor, material, and other essential resources. These systems all interrelate with the concept of data base management. In many cases, in fact most cases, the detailed data necessary to support a cost accounting system can be expected to be generated as a by-product of future automated systems supporting patient care in hospitals.

The smaller hospital should, of course, be especially concerned with the expense and complexity of having to develop and maintain a cost accounting system. There are a number of approaches that would begin to provide the benefits of such a system without having to incur the cost of automating the entire hospital. For example, the most significant element of costs, particularly in a small hospital, relates to the costs of labor. Manual or partially automated systems could be developed to focus primarily on the labor costs and productivity considerations in order to achieve partial benefits of a full-scale managerial cost accounting system. Shared data processing operations can provide an answer to the small hospital in which it might not be economically feasible to develop and maintain managerial cost accounting systems on its own. Another alternative would be through the use of service bureaus in a relationship with distributed processing and minicomputers in hospitals.

In summary, the perspective for the future is complex and will continue to change. Health care providers should continue to develop appropriate and viable responses to the challenging issues facing the field. One important way to respond is through the development and implementation of more modern, proven management techniques.

In the following chapters, the approach to cost accounting with standard costing and performance reports is detailed, specific, and practical. Hospitals can begin by implementing a basic cost information system before taking the final step toward a full cost accounting system with standards. Benefits accrue at both stages as a result of the increased control made possible by the information provided. Each hospital's management should decide its level of capability, needs, and costs and benefits of the information to be provided and then choose the system most appropriate for its purposes.

CHAPTER **2**

Cost Classification and Behavior

This chapter addresses a number of concepts that are fundamental to managerial cost accounting: cost fluctuation, fixed and variable costs, unit costs, and direct and indirect costs. These concepts of cost behavior are explained and are compared with actual cost behavior patterns. This chapter forms a foundation for the remainder of the book.

The financial manager must understand the nature of costs and their behavior in order to identify and control the cost of services and to establish the requirements providing these services. To facilitate this understanding, costs can be differentiated in several ways:

- By their relative responsiveness to changes in volume: fixed, variable, or mixed costs
- By their cost per unit of output: unit costs
- By their traceability to the object being costed: direct or indirect costs

None of these classifications is mutually exclusive. Rather, they can be used in combination to more precisely depict the behavior of a cost or a group of costs, such as variable direct costs or the fixed portion of unit costs.

Within each classification, rules exist for the further analysis and prediction of cost behavior.

FACTORS INFLUENCING COSTS

Many factors can influence the costs incurred to provide health services. The most significant factor is the volume of services provided. For example, if a hospital has low occupancy in the month of December, the cost per patient day would still be high because of high fixed costs, but total costs would be expected to decrease because of lower variable costs.

Factors other than volume also influence the costs of providing patient care. The most efficacious approach in analyzing the impact of these factors is to look at them independently, with volume held constant. Examples of a few of the many other factors that will affect costs, even though volume may be constant, are:

- **Length of stay.** If efforts are made to decrease the average length of stay of patients in a hospital, a higher cost per patient day will result. This is caused by the increased intensity of care and earlier discharge from the hospital. However, the cost per hospital stay may be lower.
- **Price of input factors.** With increases or decreases in the costs of labor, supplies, and any other expenses, the total costs and unit costs can be expected to increase or decrease correspondingly.
- **Mix of cases.** Changes in the mix of diagnoses will cause total costs to vary, because the patients' acuity level and type of illness affect the use of supplies, ancillary services, nursing services, and the average length of stay.

- **Efficiencies.** Changes in the methodology for delivering services provided by the hospital will cause costs to vary. For example, if through efficiency the radiology department can serve the same number of patients with one less radiology technician, costs will be decreased.
- **Seasonal factors.** Seasonal factors impact costs in various ways. An example of an input cost that would vary seasonally is the cost of fresh produce for the dietary department.

The above list is intended to be illustrative, not all inclusive. Other significant factors influencing costs are:

- The size and age of the hospital
- The types of pertinent services provided by the hospital
- The hospital's involvement in education and research activities
- The extent of contracts with hospital-based physicians
- The degree of hospital regulation by federal, state, and local government and third-party payers

To facilitate understanding of cost behavior as a function of volume, it is necessary to apply certain simplifying assumptions. By using the following assumptions, costs can be tracked solely in relation to activity and their fluctuations in response to volume changes can be observed:

- All costs are either fixed or variable.
- Fixed costs remain constant over the relevant range of volume.
- Variable costs vary directly with volume.
- The unit of activity is the same for all cost comparisons.
- Factors other than volume remain unchanged, so that only changes in volume affect costs.
- Cost behavior is a linear function of volume.
- Cost behavior has been accurately determined.

Total costs consist of all fixed and variable and all direct and indirect costs attributable to a cost center. The total cost curve for a cost center is shown in figure 1, below.

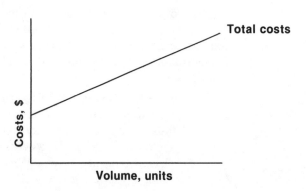

Figure 1. Total Cost Curve for a Cost Center

FIXED AND VARIABLE COSTS

In a typical business entity, costs can be classified into two different categories for a defined range of activity or volume: fixed costs and variable costs. The total cost is the sum of fixed costs plus variable costs at a given level of volume.

Fixed costs and variable costs are differentiated from one another on the basis of their responsiveness to fluctuations in volume. If a cost remains un-changed for a given time period despite wide fluctuations in activity, it is fixed; if a cost changes directly in proportion to changes in activity, it is variable.

Good examples of both types of costs can be found in the hospital's radiology department. The radiology department incurs substantial fixed costs. Typical of these costs are the depreciation of X-ray units and other equipment, salaries of the minimum staff required, and insurance. These fixed costs bear little relationship to the volume of activity within the radiology department. This example illustrates that a cost that remains constant in total, regardless of the volume of a specific activity, is a fixed cost. Fixed costs will not fluctuate over a wide range of volume over a given period. Simple fixed cost behavior is represented graphically in figure 2, below.

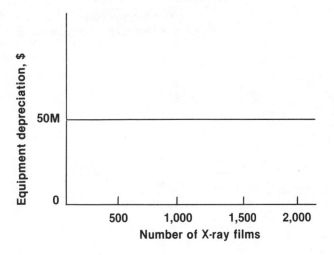

Figure 2. Fixed Costs

The radiology department also has variable costs. The cost of film is typical of a variable cost. If the cost of one film is $2, then the total cost of film used during a given period should be $2 times the number of films used during that period (assuming no spoilage, no change in input prices, and so forth). A cost that remains constant per unit of a specific activity, as in this example, is a variable cost. If all other factors are constant, a variable cost will fluctuate in direct proportion to the volume (number of units) of a specific activity. Simple variable cost behavior is illustrated graphically in figure 3, page 10.

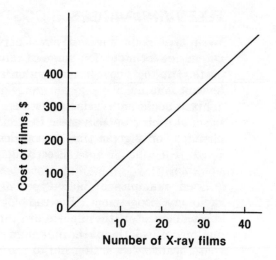

Figure 3. Variable Costs

The total cost curve, as shown in figure 4, below, can be re-examined in light of this information. Note that the fixed costs are level, whereas the variable costs increase in constant, direct proportion to increases in volume.

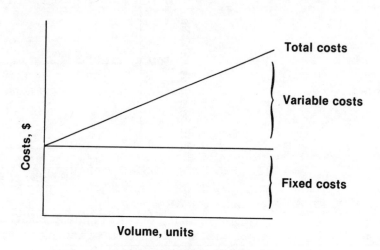

Figure 4. Total Fixed and Variable Cost Curve for a Cost Center

RELEVANT RANGES

It is not prudent to expend effort in predicting cost relationships for volumes that are improbable. The relevant range is usually a band of activity in which the hospital has had recent experience and has data on which to predict costs. As such, the use of a relevant range greatly simplifies the task of cost prediction. It should be noted that the cost behavior within the relevant range cannot be expected to continue at the extremes of no activity or great increases in activity. The effect of the relevant range on cost prediction can best be shown by example and by reference to figure 5, below. The salary expense of the business office staff might be considered a fixed cost for a 12-month period and for a range of patient volume from 50 to 85 percent of the hospital's capacity. If the patient volume exceeds 85 percent of capacity, billing and accounts receivable work loads might require the expenditure of staff overtime or addition of staff, with the attendant increase in cost. Conversely, if the patient volume falls below 50 percent of capacity, management may find it necessary to discharge some of the business office staff to reduce costs.

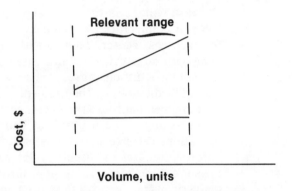

**Figure 5. Effect of Relevant Range on Total
Cost Curve for a Cost Center**

The predictions are based on the assumptions that fixed costs will remain constant within the range and that total costs can be approximated as a linear function of volume.

Another example of costs that may behave to a certain degree as fixed over a relevant range are the costs of nursing services. This is because the nature of minimum standby life-saving services, coupled with seasonal fluctuations in the number of patients treated, requires a degree of built-in excess capacity. Since there is often a problem of a tight labor market for nursing staff, laying off a nurse for a brief low-occupancy period could leave the hospital short-handed later.

In the past, labor costs in hospitals have not been sensitive to variations in service volumes and have remained fixed over a wide range of volume. Recently, however, hospitals have done much to increase the sensitivity of labor costs, by such means as the utilization of float personnel, nursing registries, and part-time staff. The behavior of labor costs is illustrated later in this chapter.

Even such fixed costs as plant and equipment can vary at extremes in volume. If patient volume declines substantially, economic forces may cause the hospital to be reduced, altered, or closed. Similarly, if patient volume reaches the hospital's physical capacity, either services will be curtailed or expansion will be required. Thus, without the use of relevant range, any cost can be shown to vary with volume. Ideally, management should understand the behavior of costs so well that it can predict variations in service volumes and the resultant effect on the incurrence of costs. Management will thereby be in a better position to increase the sensitivity of certain costs, such as nursing services, to variations in service volumes. Thus, certain fixed costs can be converted to variable costs and in this way, made subject to greater control. For example, if patient volumes can be accurately predicted, management may rely to a greater extent on part-time services instead of additional full-time nursing staff. The costs of marginal staffing requirements can thus be made a function of patient volume and become more controllable by management.

UNIT COSTS

Because volume is the most significant factor influencing the incurrence of costs, it is imperative to have an accurate measure of volume or productivity for each cost center. This measure is necessary both to establish total cost behavior and to calculate unit cost fluctuation. Although establishing units of measure is a difficult task, it is a necessary one. The choice of units of service should be dictated by the needs of managers and should be expressed in terms that are meaningful to the persons who are responsible for incurring the costs.

For example, surgical output can be measured in terms of the number of operations performed, but a more definitive measure, such as major and minor surgery, minutes of surgery, relative value units,* or a combination of these measures, might be more appropriate. Taking another example, labor and delivery output can be measured in terms of deliveries, number of patient hours in labor, or a combination of both. The key is to capture the statistical measure or group of measures that best serve as an expression of a cost center's activity. A more precise explanation of the selection and use of service units is given in chapter 4.

An understanding of unit costs is essential for many of the decisions a financial manager must make. It is useful to classify unit costs as fixed or variable, just as total costs are classified. If the unit cost is composed substantially of variable costs, then the total cost can be expected to closely reflect fluctuations in the volume of activity. Conversely, if the unit cost is composed substantially of fixed costs, then the total cost can be expected to remain constant regardless of the volume of activity. Most unit costs are composed of substantial elements of both fixed and variable costs. Therefore, analysis of unit costs for purposes of making decisions or controlling costs should identify both the fixed and variable components.

*Although there is controversy concerning the use of relative value units (RVUs) in price setting, RVUs were originally intended to reflect the effort required to provide a service. They are in use in many hospitals as standard units of measure for many departments. The use of relative value units in this text does not necessarily mean the adoption of published relative value units, but can mean an internally developed weighting system, such as the one discussed in the central supply room example in chapter 4.

The behavior of variable and fixed unit costs is illustrated in figures 6, 7, and 8, below and page 14. These figures show that the variable cost per unit stays the same over the relevant range, but the fixed cost declines as it is distributed over additional service units. The phenomenon of reduced unit costs as a result of high volume of production creates economies of scale.

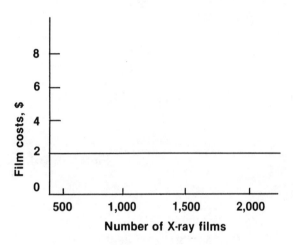

Figure 6. Variable Cost per Unit

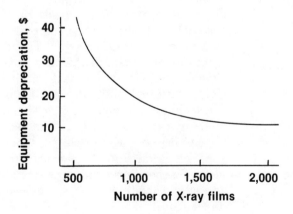

Figure 7. Fixed Cost per Unit

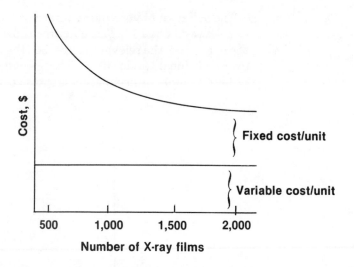

Figure 8. Total Cost per Unit

DIRECT AND INDIRECT COSTS

Another fundamental cost accounting concept is that of direct and indirect cost relationships. Direct and indirect costs are best distinguished from one another by their traceability to a specific function, cost center, or product.

In chapter 3, costs are defined as direct or indirect in terms of their relationship to patient care services. That is, if a cost is related to direct patient care, it is considered directly assignable to that patient care cost center. Costs of patient care support departments or of other nonpatient care departments are assignable to patient care centers by transfer or cost allocation techniques, which are discussed in sections II and III. Horngren states that a direct cost is one in which "there is almost always some sort of observable physical identification with the cost object that is explicitly measured in terms of the quantity of the input used, and there is no intervening basis for allocation."*

Inherent in this distinction is the concept of direct and indirect costs as they relate to a specific service or cost center within the hospital. In the housekeeping cost center, for example, the labor of housekeeping employees and cleaning supplies are direct costs even though they are indirectly related to patient services. On the other hand, repairs and maintenance services or various general and administrative services received by the housekeeping cost center are indirect costs, because a cost allocation technique is usually required to determine the cost of the services received.

The classifications of fixed and variable costs can be applied to direct and indirect costs to arrive at even more precise descriptions of cost behavior. The following example assigns some costs from the radiology department to indicate the type of costs appropriate to each cell in the matrix in figure 9, next page.

---

*Horngren, Charles T. *COST ACCOUNTING: A Managerial Emphasis*, 3rd ed. © 1972, pp. 30, 284. Adapted by permission of Prentice-Hall, Inc., Englewood Cliffs, NJ.

	Fixed	Variable
Direct	Minimum staffing	Supplies
Indirect transferred	Radiology equipment depreciation	Laundry
Indirect allocated	Administration and general	Admitting and patient accounts

**Figure 9. Sample Cost Classification
Matrix: Radiology Department**

The assignment of costs to specific cells is not a rigid procedure. Rather, it depends on the behavior of costs within a cost center, as described below. Therefore, the assignments in figure 9 should not be arbitrarily utilized for all hospitals.

- A fixed direct cost is the minimum staffing for the department. The concept of minimum level, used throughout this text, is the level of input that would be required in a department at any level of volume higher than zero, or the bottom of the relevant range. Examples of minimum levels of personnel could be a skeleton to meet requirements of the Joint Commission on Accreditation of Hospitals. In the example in figure 9, throughout the relevant range there is a minimum level of 4.2 full-time equivalent radiology technicians, 1.0 secretary, and 1.0 supervisor. These are therefore fixed direct costs.

- A fixed transferred cost is radiologic equipment depreciation, because it is accumulated in the depreciation cost center and transferred to the department at the end of the year.

- Administration and general costs include costs such as the administrator's salary, the hospital's fire insurance costs, the medical library, and the maintenance of common areas. These costs remain level over the relevant range and are allocated to inpatient areas on the basis of total patient days and to outpatient and ancillary services on a flat-percentage basis.

- A variable direct cost in the radiology department is supplies. In this category are the costs of film, developer, and other diagnostic and office supplies. The use of these supplies varies directly with the volume of patients. Laundry costs are charged to radiology on a per-piece basis. Each patient uses a gown, and drapes are used for some special procedures. These costs therefore also vary directly as a result of variations in volume.

- The admitting and patient accounts department costs are allocated to patient care departments on some equivalent basis as an allocated indirect variable cost.

REFINEMENTS OF COST BEHAVIOR

The concepts discussed thus far provide an understanding of the relative impact of volume on total costs and unit costs and the further classification of the traceability of a cost to the final product or activity. The assumptions introduced were necessary to develop these concepts, but need to be relaxed to account for the array of cost behavior that a financial manager can expect to encounter. Refinement of the concepts of fixed and variable costs and a brief discussion of mixed costs will provide a more complete understanding of cost behavior patterns.

Variable Cost Patterns

Variable costs have been defined as those that vary in constant direct proportion to volume. In reality, however, most costs that vary with volume do not vary in direct proportion to the services rendered. If costs are not precisely predictable, it becomes more challenging for the financial manager to budget and control cost. It is helpful, therefore, to be aware of other common cost behavior patterns. A common variable cost pattern in hospitals is the step variable pattern.

Earlier, labor costs were shown to have some of the qualities of a fixed cost. This is due to the fact that hospital labor costs commonly follow a step variable pattern. Consider the case of a nursing floor with 20 beds. There may be a necessary minimum staff of three per shift: one RN, one LPN, and one nursing assistant. As the patient census increases, or the patient mix changes, or special programs are added, more nursing personnel will be required. This results in the nursing cost behavior pattern illustrated in figure 10, below.

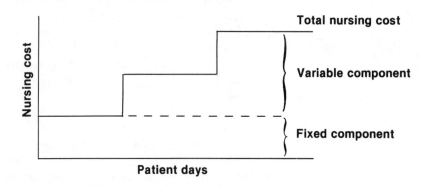

Figure 10. Step Variable Cost Curve

The step variable pattern is a result of the inability to hire small, very responsive units of labor. Often, nursing floors add staff only by adding permanent full-time employees, rather than utilizing part-time, temporary, or floating staff during peak periods. This would bring the line closer to a standard variable cost line by increasing the responsiveness of labor costs to volume and improving control.

The step variable pattern is further confused by the impact of such factors as the mix of services required and the illness levels of the patients as they affect the level of labor required. In reality, the labor cost line will look more like the graph in figure 11, below.

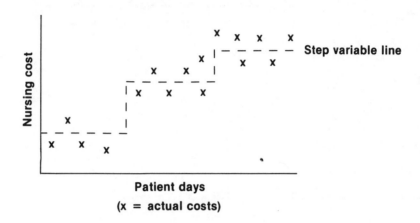

Figure 11. Actual Labor Costs

While the step variable cost makes the tasks of accurate prediction and financial control more difficult, they can still be accomplished by the use of some reasonable assumptions. For example, if the unit is a homogeneous unit, such as coronary care, in which the services provided are determined by protocol, the service mix can be assumed to be unchanging. Also, there might be a relatively stable mix of the severity of illness on the unit, and so the patient mix can be assumed to be stable.

The budget line shown in figure 12, below, is based on these assumptions. When compared with actual cost, it does an excellent job of prediction, despite the many factors impacting costs besides volume. Thus, the cost relationship may be a step variable pattern, but a straight line can be assumed.

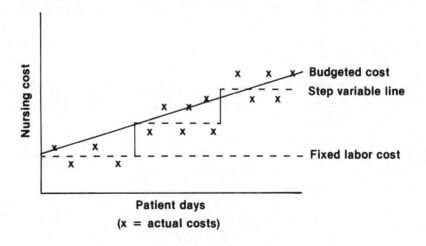

Figure 12. Actual Labor Costs and Budget Line

The other major variable expense category in hospitals is supplies. Ideally, supplies are consumed as a result of the volume of patient days in the hospital — a direct variable pattern. However, efficiency, price of input factors, and intensity of services, for example, impact supply costs in addition to number of patient days. The actual costs will vary directly with volume, but cannot be expected to exactly follow the budget line. This is illustrated in figure 13, below.

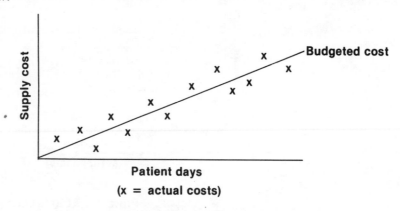

Figure 13. Actual Supply Costs and Budget Line

To gain an understanding of the cost behavior of supplies and to control costs of supplies, an analysis on a department-by-department basis is essential. The behavior patterns for supplies in individual departments may not be influenced by as wide a mix of variables. The service volume related to supply consumption in individual departments will therefore be more predictable.

For example, maintenance supplies will be variable, but may have no relationships to the volume of patient services rendered. Supplies consumed for maintenance will be affected by the age of the equipment in use and the age of the hospital structure. Nevertheless, most hospitals can determine behaviors for maintenance on the basis of historical data. Also, hospital policy can establish the rate at which routine maintenance is performed: rooms repainted every three years, light bulbs replaced every eight months, and so forth. As was shown in the labor cost example, the lack of a precisely predictable pattern of cost behavior does not preclude control.

Fixed Cost Patterns

In the earlier treatment of fixed costs, they were presented to be constant in total over a period of time and with little or no variability. Fixed costs represent costs incurred to provide the capacity necessary to render hospital services, but are unrelated, in the short run, to volume. Therefore, fixed costs should be the easiest to control. For example, control can be exerted over certain types of fixed costs called discretionary costs. Fixed costs can be classified into two categories:

- *Sunk costs,* such as plant depreciation, which, once committed, are absolute over a period of time and will remain fixed at a specific level until capacity is reached.
- *Discretionary costs,* such as insurance, which remain fixed over periodic volume changes, but can be altered from period to period by

management decision. Other discretionary costs are legal fees, research expenditures, training expenditures, and audit fees.

It should be recognized that these expenditures may at times vary in total, though not in direct relation to the volume of services. In many situations, management may, at its discretion, alter one or more of these costs from year to year without a material effect on the volume or quality of service.

Fixed costs, therefore, will not remain constant from year to year, because of several reasons:

- Additions to plant and equipment unrelated to maintenance of plant or volume, such as the addition of new technology
- Management action on discretionary costs
- Changes in depreciation schedules, both in terms of changes in useful lives and the expiration of fixed assets

An example of a fixed cost curve is shown in figure 14, below.

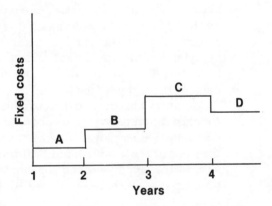

Figure 14. Fixed Cost Curve

Figure 14 shows four years of fixed costs. In year 1, the depreciation for the year was level A. In year 2, a piece of radiologic equipment with a 10-year useful life was added, bringing total fixed costs to level B. In year 3, malpractice insurance increased greatly, and total fixed costs rose to level C. In year 4, the fixed costs dropped to level D as depreciation was reduced as a result of the expiration of some fixed assets.

Mixed Behavior Patterns   It is also necessary to briefly address those costs that have both fixed and variable components. The example of labor costs has already been presented. Another common cost with a mixed behavior pattern is utilities costs. Utilities usually have a fixed minimum charge and a charge that is variable above the minimum. Also, there is a lower rate for very high-volume users. This cost behavior is represented by figure 15, next page.

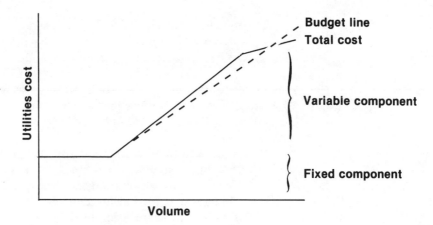

Figure 15. Utilities Cost Curve and Budget Line

The lack of a direct proportionate relationship over the entire cost line does not preclude either budgeting or control, as actual costs are well approximated by the budget line. The budget line is developed by separating the known fixed component and the variable component (equalling rate times volume) and applying knowledge of fixed and variable costs to predict the behavior of the total cost line. Costs with mixed behavior patterns are dealt with in this manner throughout this book.

Costs may also behave in a curvilinear manner. An example of such behavior could be the employer's share of payroll taxes. The total cost is variable up to a maximum per employee. Payroll taxes will vary according to total payroll, and the slope of the total cost curve at the end of the year will depend on the salary level of the employees and the employee turnover during the year. This relationship is represented in figure 16, below.

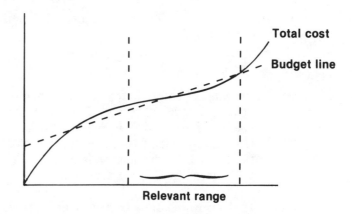

Figure 16. Payroll Cost Curve and Budget Line

Again, the budget line, although linear, is a close approximation to the total cost curve within the relevant range. Since the amount of costs that behave in a curvilinear manner are not material in hospitals, the linear approximation is sufficient for management's needs.

SUMMARY

In summary, most costs can be classified as either fixed or variable, but some costs behave in a manner that makes them difficult to categorize strictly. Fixed and variable unit costs behave in manners distinct from one another. A variable cost in total will tend to vary in proportion to the volume of a specific activity. Fixed costs in total will tend to remain constant throughout a relevant range of activity. As volume approaches the extremes of this relevant range, fixed costs may become variable. If the financial manager can accurately determine the relevant range of activity and reasonably predict the service volumes, then he can exercise some control over fixed costs and take advantage of opportunities to convert fixed costs to variable costs.

A unit of measure used to determine a volume of activity must bear a close relationship to cost incurrence. The unit of measure should also be expressed in terms meaningful to those responsible for incurring costs.

In identifying the cost of services, direct costs have a direct observable identification with the service and can be explicitly measured in terms of the quantity of services. Indirect costs have only indirect relationships, and identification with specific services requires cost allocation techniques.

The understanding of cost behavior is essential to cost identification, budgeting, and planning. Costs should be analyzed to the level of detail necessary to determine a reasonable cost relationship with volume of services rendered. The cost accounting system presented in section III enables managers of all levels to identify, predict, present, analyze, and control costs. The strict variable and fixed definitions of cost behavior are necessary to understand the system even though they do not always coincide with actual cost behavior. When the financial manager understands cost behavior, he can utilize known alternative behavior patterns to analyze and predict costs.

SECTION II.
BASIC COST INFORMATION SYSTEM

CHAPTER **3**

Overview of Basic Cost Information

The principles discussed in chapter 2 are the foundation for hospital cost accounting. The overall objective of cost accounting is to determine accurately and efficiently all costs required to provide each of the hospital's services; a computation of total aggregate cost for all such services is not sufficient. For managers to effectively plan, evaluate, and exercise control over their departments, detailed cost and volume data are required.

As mandated by third-party payers, most hospitals are presently using cost finding to allocate all indirect and support costs to revenue centers. The step-down or double-apportionment methods determine department costs in a crude, aggregate basis and are often performed only once per year. Therefore, these methods do not provide managers with information that is sufficiently detailed and timely to assist them in the task of control.

This book presents two levels of cost accounting. In this section, a basic cost information system without standards is presented. This system is an improvement over current cost-finding methods, but does not provide sufficient information for the creation of flexible budgeting, performance reporting, and variance analysis. In section III, a cost accounting system is presented. The cost accounting refinements outlined provide for accurate and timely generation of all the management reports mentioned above. This system is the ideal toward which hospitals should strive and requires the use of engineered standards.

In the 1970s, there were only a few hospitals in the United States that utilized cost accounting systems. These systems are well worth the effort required to develop and maintain them, for the benefits from the implementation of a cost accounting system are many:

- It generates the information required for managers to analyze costs in relation to cost centers, diagnoses, patients, research efforts, and educational endeavors.
- It provides managers with timely, flexible performance reports that use standards to measure the effectiveness of their departments, cost centers, or functions.
- It develops information to assist managers in evaluating the impact of such factors as seasonality, changes in case mix, and changes in efficiency.
- It provides detailed cost information by service unit, which can be used in negotiations with regulatory agencies on rate review, prospective budgeting and other reimbursement limitation mechanisms.
- It creates the information required to develop hospitalwide pricing policies on basis of the actual costs of services provided.

To develop both systems, several accounting techniques need be applied.

The first is the matching process, which relates all costs to the revenues that are generated by their incurrence. The matching process identifies costs by cost center, department, point of service, or service unit. Further analysis by natural expense classification, such as salaries, supplies, or professional fees, is also possible.

To implement the matching process technique, certain key features are required:

- All costs incurred should be recorded accurately in the correct time period.
- All elements of cost (labor, supplies, and so forth) should be distributed and recorded in the appropriate cost center that reflects the point of service.
- Appropriate service units should be identified in each cost center so that the volume of a provided service can be measured.
- All costs should be matched with the service units to compute accurate unit costs.

Hospital financial accounting systems play an important role in cost accounting. The payroll and labor distribution system is one of the most important sources of financial and statistical information for cost determination. Similarly, the purchasing system, fixed asset system, and inventory and cost transfer system provide necessary information to determine total costs for all units. In essence, both financial and statistical accounting systems provide the accumulation of costs that are matched against appropriate measurement units in order to evaluate performance on the basis of managerial responsibility.

Once established and implemented, cost accounting provides management with sufficient managerial information to:

- Take advantage of opportunities to convert the behavior of fixed costs (especially labor) to that of variable costs and thus avoid critical cash shortages created by downturns in volume
- Document costs in a manner that can be used by management to evaluate and select appropriate cost-saving steps and to present well-founded justification for necessary rate increases
- Evaluate performance in all departments on a periodic basis and take corrective action before problems are out of control
- Utilize financial data more effectively as part of the planning process
- Achieve these objectives without sacrificing the quality of service provided or, at least, with full knowledge of the appropriate interface between quality and efficiency

Existing text materials in cost accounting generally classify cost accounting systems as either process costing or job order costing. Standard costing may or may not be employed in either approach. Even though cost accounting is often considered less effective without standards, for instructional purposes of this text, the following elements of a basic information system without standards will be presented in this section:

- *Process costing* is the most commonly used in organizations that have to continually process a homogeneous product or service. It is an averaging system that accumulates costs according to specific processes (cost centers). As each cost center completes the specific process, the system assigns unit costs, which are added to the product or service.

- *Job order costing* is a system used to accumulate costs for products or services that vary considerably from order to order. Like the process costing system, it uses averaging to a certain degree, but it relies more on the specific identification of resources used to produce individual product units or job lots.

Hospitals provide patients with a wide range of services in an almost endless variety of combinations. Of the two costing systems, the theoretical ideal in a hospital is a job order system, in which the specific cost applied to each patient would be identified. The job order system centers around the designation of costs according to diagnosis category. The cost of treating each patient would be computed on the basis of actual service units, drugs, and supplies applied to his care. This would provide the following advantages:

- Individual patient care could be priced in relation to the cost of providing it.
- Physicians could know the cost implications to their patients for each added service.
- Management and physicians could relate costs to established norms of care and could establish ranges of acceptable costs by diagnosis.
- Management could analyze the impact of changes in case mix.
- Cost versus benefit considerations could be a part of the decision to use a specific procedure.
- Management could demonstrate the impact of treating patients from different payer classes.

A job order system by patient appears to be the theoretical ideal for the hospital setting. There are, however, significant practical constraints involved in its implementation under conditions present in modern hospitals. The system described here is intended to be a practical application: a hybrid that combines features of both process costing and job order systems. It will move hospitals closer to the development of a patient-by-patient cost accounting system and, in the interim, will provide for performance measurement on the existing departmental or cost center basis. With this system, emphasis will be placed on identification of the costs of all units of service delivered to the patient, both directly and indirectly, from each cost center in the hospital. This will allow cost control on a departmental basis in a system that is similar to process costing. It will also provide a beginning for the development of a data base that will allow conversion to the job order system in the future.

Hospital departments and cost centers have cost behavior patterns and operating relationships that permit them to be categorized into five types:

- Routine patient care departments or cost/revenue centers
- Ancillary patient care departments or cost/revenue centers
- Patient care support departments or cost centers
- General and administrative departments or cost centers
- Nonpatient care departments or cost centers

The first four types of departments exist for the purpose of either providing health care services or providing necessary support to other departments that do provide health care services. The fifth type is for nonrelated hospital activities such as research or community activity and is addressed in chapter 7. For instructional purposes, it will be assumed that expenses should be recorded in the four types of patient care-related departments. Assignments will be made in accordance with the following three basic premises:

1. All expenses incurred will initially be assigned and recorded directly

to a cost center. If this cost center is directly involved in patient care, the expense assignment, called *direct costing,* is complete, and the expenses will be referred to as direct expenses.

2. Expenses of patient care support departments, which provide services to other departments, will be transferred accordingly. This secondary expense assignment will be called *transfer costing,* and these expenses will be referred to as transferred expenses.

3. Departmental expenses that cannot be identified as directly applicable to patient care services or support services will be allocated to other departments. This expense assignment will be called *cost allocation,* and these expenses will be referred to as allocated expenses.

All expenses should be distributed by specific identification, indirect identification or a reasonable allocation process to some cost center in which managerial responsibility can be established. The process to accomplish this will differ from department to department. It should be noted, however, that, in each case, cost allocations will be kept to a minimum.

To some extent, the processes that occur in a hospital can be likened to a production operation. The following is a characterization of how patient care departments are responsible for the day-to-day care of patients and serve as the primary contact point with patients.

From a cost accounting standpoint, albeit theoretical, each service provided to a patient can be accounted for on a job order sheet. Nursing units or other patient care departments are processing centers because they order services from ancillary patient care departments and then record such services on job sheets. Radiology and laboratory departments perform diagnostic examinations of patients and advise the physician and processing center of their findings. Other ancillary departments, such as the operating room, provide services to correct patients' problems and provide diagnostic data from exploratory procedures. Pharmacy and central supply provide drugs and materials to be administered by the processing centers. They also supply patient care materials to other departments, such as surgical packs for use in the operating room. Dietary, medical records, and housekeeping departments are examples of patient care support departments that provide services to the job processing centers and the ancillary departments. They can provide services directly applied to patients, such as food from the dietary department, or can provide support services necessary for patient care, such as medical records and housekeeping.

In addition to the direct departmental expenses and the direct service or supply expenses transferred from support departments, indirect general and administrative overhead is incurred. This direct overhead, often referred to as *burden,* usually cannot be identified with specific services rendered by patient care departments or patient support departments. Therefore, it must be allocated on some reasonable basis.

CHAPTER 4

Selection and Use of Service Units

As discussed in chapter 2, any cost accounting system requires a measure of productivity or volume for each cost center. Establishing measurement units for each service rendered to patients, transferred to other departments, or prepared for inventory allows costs to be expressed in relation to levels of production or service provided. Computing unit costs of services provided will help management determine appropriate prices for services. It will also serve as the basis for evaluations of departmental efficiency and will provide a means by which the unit cost of services provided by support departments can be related more directly to patient care.

The selection of an appropriate service unit should be based on the following criteria:

- It should be the single factor that most clearly causes the particular department's cost to vary. For example, the total number of X-ray exams given will, in the long run, be most closely related to the resources consumed.
- It should be easily understood or recognized: production units must be measurable. Goals such as extension of life or complete restoration of health are valid, but difficult to quantify. The service unit should be measurable on a periodic basis and should be consistent enough to be meaningful to the responsible manager or supervisor.
- It should be primarily affected by volume. This concept is important but often misunderstood. For example, the number of X-ray exams is a better measure of production volume than the number of X-ray films consumed, because the number of exams completed is the real service volume of the department. Inefficient use of film could be recorded far in excess of the number of completed exams. In addition, management decisions to change a film supplier or discard supplies are not necessarily affected by service volume. Productivity should be measured only by services delivered, not by other factors.

Because productivity is difficult to measure in many hospital departments, it may be the largest single impediment to the implementation of cost accounting. Hospitals have been slow in attempting to install production and cost measurement systems. The difficulty of quantification, however, should not preclude moving forward and gaining the ability to measure and control operating costs. Service units should be established for each direct and indirect cost center that renders services. Although some compromise may be required in choosing units of measure, the objective of cost accounting is to develop the best service units available for each department and to match costs with those units. Examples of suggested service units for selected departments are:

Department	Service units
Emergency	Number of visits Time
Physical therapy	Number of treatments Modalities
Nursery	Patient days
Labor and delivery	Number of births Minutes of labor
Surgery	Operations Major and minor operations Patient minutes in surgery Time-team concept
Laboratory	Number of tests College of American Pathologists' units
Radiology	Number of exams Relative value units

Admittedly, these examples are very basic. A more comprehensive set of suggested service units should be developed on the basis of the hospital's needs. In developing service units, consideration should be given to:

- The size of the department measured
- The complexity of the department measured
- The cost of recording and counting the service units and the benefits derived

It should be emphasized that the development of a statistical accounting system is predicated on the effective participation of departmental personnel. Therefore, the training and appropriate placement of staff is of the utmost importance.

For example, for a hospital attempting to develop service units for surgery, the easiest measure to develop would be the number of operations, because this relates to the costs, causes costs to vary, is easily understood, and is a measure of volume. It may be an ineffective measure, however, if the mix of operations (complexity, length of time required, resources used to perform) varies from month to month. Department personnel can measure surgical volume better by dividing operations into subclassifications, such as major and minor. Different weights would be applied to each type of operation and multiplied by the volume to arrive at the total service units. Further sophistication could be added by recording minutes of surgery. This could overcome some of the mix change effects, but may be harder for staff to record accurately. Relative value units could be applied to all operations to gain added sophistication, but this would make the task of recording and implementing more difficult.

The question at hand is one of materiality. Is the chance of error or misstatement of volume great enough to justify the added effort to implement such a system? How much more control can be achieved by adding sophistication to the system? In small, uncomplicated departments, simple or even crude measures of volume may be sufficient. The deciding factor should be the level of refinement required by management to exercise an appropriate level of control. Admittedly, this is a somewhat subjective judgment.

One point should be stressed in this discussion: cost identificaton systems and methods need to be tailored to individual hospital situations. Hospital complexity and the mix of services rendered are significantly different from hospital to hospital. Therefore, the ability to measure and compare cost data is neither furthered nor enhanced by forcing a rigid set of rules on all hospitals. Common principles and criteria form the connecting thread among institutions.

The following is an example of the determination and application of service units to a department. The controller of a 200-bed general acute care hospital is working with the general stores manager to develop a service unit for the department's functions. He needs this to measure the performance level in the stores department and to transfer the expense of operating the stores department to the user departments in the hospital. The stores manager informed the controller that the following activities are performed in the general stores department.

- As shipments and deliveries of supplies are received, receiving reports are prepared for each.
- Supplies are stacked on the storage shelves.
- Inventory cards for receipts from vendors and transfers to user departments are posted for 60% of all inventory items. This assists staff in maintaining control of inventory levels. The rest of the items stocked are checked on a periodic basis.
- Twice a week, floor stocks of general supplies are restocked to a predetermined level by stores personnel.
- Daily requisitions of stores items are filled and delivered to other departments in the hospital.
- A full-time clerk in the stores department maintains inventory cards, transmits receiving reports to accounting, and handles the clerical functions connected with summarizing transfers to other departments.

Which of the activities listed could be measured and recorded to best fit the criteria for a valid measure of service? The primary function of the department is to receive, store, and transfer supplies consumed by the hospital. Which unit causes costs to vary? For the most part, the cost of operations is stable. Because this stores department is not large or complex, most of its costs are relatively final, although the volume of shipments or requisitions filled may cause overtime or an increase in the use of clerical manpower. Two key questions become important:

- What service unit best relates to services rendered to other departments?
- What service unit best relates to any increase in the cost of operating the stores department?

The controller and the stores manager determine that the transfer of stores expense to user departments is the most critical element in this case. They decide that, as there are two possible measures of the transfer to other departments, the degree of detail is in question: Should the number of requisitions filled be the measure, or rather should it be the number of requisition line items? Since the simplest to record is the number of requisitions, the controller decides to use this as his measure. He therefore tests the number of requisitions filled against the selection criteria to determine its appropriateness. His analysis is as follows:

- The number of requisitions filled relates to the cost-causing factors because the greatest number of man-hours is spent filling requisitions and restocking user department floor stock.
- The number of requisitions filled is easily counted by a clerk, who can log the number processed daily.
- The number of requisitions filled relates to the volume of all activities in the stores department. The more requisitions filled, the more shipments received and the more turnover of stock.

One element is unaccounted for by this measure: volume. Volume is also affected by the amount of supplies delivered to restock the departmental floor stocks. Because this is a routine function, the controller decides that he will ignore this measure and check his computations for reasonableness quarterly. If he has reason to believe this function changes in relation to the requisition activity, he will attempt to measure the restocking activity, assign a weight to those deliveries, and add that to his volume measurement units next year.

With this decision made, he submits a written procedure to the manager that requires the stores clerk to complete the form illustrated in figure 17, below.

STORES DEPARTMENT
LOG OF REQUISITIONS FILLED
MONTH ENDING _____

Date	Nursing floors	Number of requisitions filled			Other hospital departments		Total
		Admitting	X-ray	Lab			
1st	X	X	X	X	X	X	XXX
2nd							
31st							
Totals	XX	XX	XX	XX	XX	XX	XXXXXX

Figure 17. Stores Department Log of Requisitions Filled

Figure 17 is an illustration of the logic applied in developing service units. The decision reached in the example demonstrates the mix of the ideal and pragmatic considerations that enter into each situation. Unfortunately, many departments are more complex than the stores function.

Consider another example. The controller is now preparing to establish service units for the central supply room (sterile supply). The department manager informs the controller that the following activities are performed:

- IVs are stored and distributed to the nursing floors.
- Sterile packs and disposables are stored and distributed to the nursing floors and ancillary departments on an ongoing basis.
- Minor equipment, surgical packs, and trays for ancillary and nursing floors are assembled and sterilized.
- Minor equipment, surgical packs, and trays are stored and distributed upon request.
- The department has personnel that perform the storage function and the sterilizing function and record the distribution of materials and trays.
- In addition to the above, some of the trays and solutions distributed are charged directly to the patient's account by personnel in the central supply room (CSR). The CSR thus has both patient revenue and transfers to other departments to record.

Which of the activities listed is the primary service of the CSR? The controller determines that two functions are performed: one is a storage function similar to that performed by the general stores, and the other is an assembly and distribution function performed on the surgical supplies and trays. There is a need to divide the CSR into two subdepartments or functions with a unit of measure for each.

The controller decides to use the number of requisitions filled as the unit of measure for the storage function. The same form developed in the stores department will be used to record activity. The assembly function for surgical supplies and trays is more complex. All expenses charged to CSR will have to be identified and allocated between the two functions. The assembly function has a distinct production characteristic and will be a labor added product as the final production unit. If carried to the extreme, this could mean accounting for raw materials, work in process, and finished goods. The finished goods would then be transferred on a fully costed basis to the user departments and to a cost of goods sold account for items charged directly to patients. The controller recognizes this as the ideal solution for the measurement of this function, but realizes his hospital does not currently have the accounting resources to implement this system.

He considers the following as a possible alternative:

- All trays and surgical packs will be classified by complexity to prepare on a relative value unit scale of 1 to 10.
- A record will be kept of the number of value units sent to each department and charged to patients.
- The total service units for the CSR assembly function will be the value units transferred and charged.

The controller thinks that only minimal distortion in the unit cost computation will result, as the department manager assures him that the inventory of finished trays remains fairly stable at all times. The units transferred and charged will therefore be very close to the units assembled in a given period. The controller decides to accept this on a trial basis and to check the finished units inventory on a periodic basis in the coming year to verify his assumption. The same form used for the general supply function will be used to record volume, but value units will be recorded instead of the number of items transferred and charged.

In summary, the measurement of output for each hospital department, cost center, or function is essential to proper cost accounting. The determination of effectiveness and efficiency are dependent upon the ability to measure service volume (output). The fact that a hospital has a vast array of services that are not homogeneous should not preclude development of this valuable tool. Each department should record output with that factor or group of factors that most closely measures the causes of costs to vary and is easily understood and accumulated.

CHAPTER 5

Direct Costing

This chapter discusses the techniques used to accumulate and account for costs initially identified with a department or cost center. It describes the different types of direct expenses incurred in a hospital and the fundamental procedures for assigning and initially recording the expense to specific cost centers. Each segment of the accounting system that has a role in the basic cost information system is examined.

All costs incurred should ultimately be assigned or attributed to the output, results, or achievements of the organization and its activities. This is necessary for the basic cost information system to identify the cost of providing each type of service. All costs incurred should be matched with the individual department or cost center responsible for incurring the cost. Following the initial cost determination on a responsibility basis, costs should be related to specific functions on a service unit basis within the department or cost center.

The elements required to implement direct costing are as follows:

- A method of identifying expenses by natural expense classification and by responsibility center or function—*chart of accounts*
- A method of accounting for and distributing all personnel expenses to the actual areas in which employees' time was spent—*payroll and labor distribution system*
- A method of determining and distributing all nonsalary direct expenses within the hospital—*purchasing system*
- A method of amortizing deferred expenses and matching them with services rendered—*deferred expense amortization system*
- A method of transferring the cost of stored or processed goods and supplies from support departments to user departments—*inventory and cost transfer system.*

Following the discussion of these elements is a presentation of performance reporting based only on direct departmental costs. This performance report is very basic and will be refined later in this section as transferred and allocated costs are added to the system.

CHART OF ACCOUNTS

Costs are to be separated into various classifications. For this purpose, the chart of accounts plays an important role in cost accounting.

No specific chart of accounts is recommended. However, the chart should be sufficiently detailed to identify individual managerial units. The chart can be adapted to the unique needs of each hospital. It identifies expense by responsibility center and natural expense classification and can be expanded to provide functional identification.

Natural expense classifications should be used to subdivide costs by types. The major classifications of expenses are: salaries and wages, employee benefits, professional fees, medical and surgical supplies, nonmedical and non-surgical supplies, purchased services, utilities, other direct expenses, depreciation, and rent.

Because these natural classifications are general, there are subclassifications within each natural classification. The level of subclassification used depends on the size, complexity, and needs of the individual institution. The materiality of an individual expense in relation to the total expense of a cost center and the overall dollar volume of expenses within a cost center should be the primary consideration. Cost analysis is most accurate when each expense item is identified at the lowest level deemed appropriate within the natural classification. For example, medical and surgical supplies could be subclassified as follows:

- Prostheses
- General surgical supplies
- Anesthetic materials
- Oxygen and other medical gases
- IV solutions
- Pharmaceuticals
- Radioactive materials
- Radioactive films
- Other medical care materials and supplies

The cost center responsible for incurring any of the supply costs listed would be charged with the expense identified at the subclassification level indicated. For instance, pharmacy can include pharmaceuticals, IV solutions, and other medical care materials and supplies. Radiology can include radioactive materials, radiology film, and other medical care materials and supplies. Salaries and wages can be identified by major category of employee within each cost center.

Three considerations are necessary to determine the cost center responsible for an item of expense:

- The department that ordered the goods or services
- The point of use of the goods or services
- The manager who has control over the application of the goods or services

PAYROLL AND LABOR DISTRIBUTION SYSTEM

Payroll is the largest single part of a hospital's operating expenses. Therefore, accurate labor distribution and accounting of all payroll expense are the most important steps in the cost accounting process. Labor cost should be matched with services performed. The labor cost for personnel that serve more than one cost center is distributed among the cost centers served. Movement from cost center to cost center by an employee must be recorded to all cost centers to achieve proper distribution.

In addition to the identification of proper employee location and time, it is important that the cost of payroll expense be determined. Employee benefits, including vacation, holiday, and sick pay, are part of labor cost. A method for distributing employee benefits with labor and salary expense is a necessary part of the cost accounting system.

The labor distribution system used to match labor cost with services rendered to patients or to other cost centers is relatively simple for those cost centers whose assigned employees spent 100 percent of their time working in their assigned cost center. Their salaries and benefits are charged to expense in their departments. Their benefits will be accrued as earned and charged to expense in proportion to salaries incurred for actual time worked.

PURCHASING SYSTEM   Vendors

The need for a well-defined and controlled purchasing system is readily apparent when consideration is given to the wide range of supplies and services a hospital purchases, such as drugs, medical supplies, instruments, minor equipment, laundry and linen, consultants, attorneys, auditors, data processing, various educational conferences, utilities, and insurance.

It is common to find hospitals with a well-defined and controlled centralized purchasing function that excludes some significant purchases. For example, food and drugs may be purchased directly from vendors. Regardless of the degree of centralization or the type of purchasing or materials management system used, the system should include the following control elements:

- Purchase requisitions issued by department managers to the purchasing officer or the stores manager for goods normally held in inventory
- Purchase orders issued to vendors with copies to the receiving department and accounts payable department
- Receiving reports issued for goods received and identifying the number of units received
- Audit function, matching invoices, purchase orders, and receiving reports, to ensure that goods and services are properly approved, received, and priced
- Identification, coding, and charging of all supplies, services, and expenses by natural expense classification to the responsible department or cost center
- Purchasing system control over services ordered directly from vendors, such as temporary employees from manpower agencies, contract physician services, outside laboratory services, and legal and accounting services
- The charging to inventory or the prepaid expense of goods or services to be consumed in future accounting periods as appropriate and expensed as consumed

The purchasing system should match the cost of each item with the cost center responsible for its use, so that each responsible manager is charged with the proper share of cost. It is also important to remember that the appropriate expense must be matched against the service units to measure the accurate unit cost of services provided.

AMORTIZATION OF ASSETS AND DEFERRED EXPENSES

Costs recorded on balance sheets represent expenses that are deferred to be matched with services to be rendered in the future. The most significant deferred expense is the investment in the hospital plant and equipment. Others include prepaid expenses such as insurance, service contracts, interest, taxes, and other prepaid items. Unamortized borrowing costs and preopening costs in capital expansion or renovation programs are also examples of deferred expenses.

A method of matching deferred expenses with services rendered must be developed for each deferred expense item. Development of the method should include the following criteria:

- The method should consider the time period during which the item will be consumed and the most appropriate method of matching consumption with services rendered.
- The depreciation of hospital plant and equipment should be recognized through amortization of the original cost over its estimated useful life.
- The selected method of depreciation needs to relate as nearly as possible to the use of the asset. For instance, the depreciation of X-ray equipment may be based on the number of tests the equipment could reasonably be expected to perform during its life. Hours of service rendered could also be used to amortize the equipment's cost.
- Depreciation of equipment cost should be charged to the cost center using the equipment. This will require the maintenance of detailed equipment records that show the department using the equipment and the amount of depreciation charged. The equipment records will also be required to record transfers of equipment from cost center to cost center. An equipment requisition system is often used by management to assist them in maintaining control of equipment.
- Depreciation of buildings should be charged to the using cost centers based on the area they occupy.
- Special cost areas need to be separately identified and related amortization charged directly to the using cost center. Special cost areas could include leaded walls in Radiology and special floors and cooling systems for electronic data processing equipment. Common areas can be apportioned by dropping them from the space used to determine cost per square foot.
- Prepaid expenses, unamortized borrowing costs, capitalized leases, and preopening costs should be amortized by using generally accepted accounting methods. The method of amortization is generally determined by the nature of the prepaid item. For further information on amortization methods for capitalized leases, consult authoritative accounting literature.
- After the amount of amortization has been estimated for each deferred expense, the service to which it relates needs to be identified so that costs can be properly matched. Prepaid service contracts should be amortized to the center receiving the service.

INVENTORY AND COST TRANSFER SYSTEM

Cost accounting requires an inventory control and charge subsystem to transfer the cost of goods and supplies from the inventory holding or central stores department to the user departments for further processing, consumption, or sale to patients. The specific transfer method used is of secondary importance as long as the identification of usage is accurate.

Matching the proper cost center with the cost of all materials and supplies consumed is of primary importance. A requisition form should be required to order any material and supply item from stores, and the cost should be charged to the user department. Because the cost identification process starts in the inventory and stores function, the cost of operating this function should also be transferred to the user departments.

An orderly, systematic inventory record system is required. Last-in first-out, or first-in first-out, and average cost are all applicable, depending on the hospital's needs. In any event, a decision has to be made to commit hospital resources to maintaining the data necessary to properly control and account for stores.

Charging the cost of the stores function to the user is difficult, as indicated in chapter 4. However, once a unit of measurement is selected, the process is simplified.

In the example in chapter 4, the number of requisitions filled was determined to be a good measure of the general stores department function. To further refine this example, the following process is suggested.

If the hospital's cost accumulation system is current and provides total actual expense for the stores department on a timely basis, a monthly summary of charges can be made to transfer all costs of operating the department to user departments on the basis of service units (requisitions filled, in the example).

If the actual cost accumulation is not available on a timely basis, an estimated transfer can be made as follows:

- Labor and other support costs can be estimated for the year, as most hospitals do through development of their budgets. At the same time costs are being estimated, the number of requisitions filled would also be estimated for the year.
- Using this information, the cost of each requisition filled (unit value) can be estimated for the next year. As the new year progresses, the estimated cost of the stores function is transferred to the user departments by applying that unit value to the cost of each requisition.

These applied estimated costs should be compared or matched with the actual costs to establish the variances that may occur. The manager of the stores function should explain the variances, thus allowing management to exercise further control over the operation and show any deficiencies.

The variances should be accounted for on at least a quarterly basis, although monthly analysis is preferred. This can be done through the use of transfer accounts. For example, see figure 18, next page.

Central supply is another function that provides materials and supplies to user departments. However, central supply not only receives material from general stores for transfer to patient service centers, but also performs a production function. Packs and trays are assembled by central supply for use in the operating, emergency, and delivery rooms. Cost accounting requires that the labor and other departmental support cost of preparing the packs and trays be included with the cost of materials to determine the proper cost to transfer. Periodic computation of the unit cost of all materials handled or prepared by central supply is required. The unit costs are then transferred to the user departments on the basis of actual units transferred. This is done on a summary basis at the end of each measurement period.

In addition to packs and trays, there are many other services rendered by the support departments for patient care departments or other support and administrative cost centers, such as housekeeping and maintenance services. If fully costed, these services include all direct labor and material costs, including related overhead, all costs transferred from other cost centers, and a portion of general and administrative overhead. The process of full costing is covered in chapter 6.

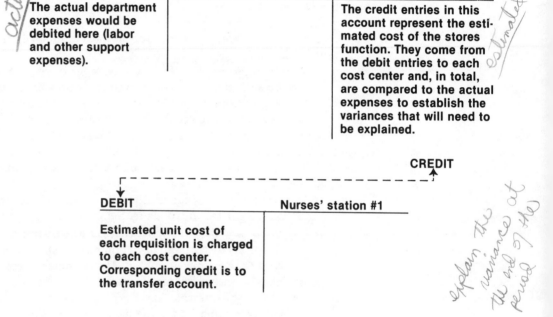

Figure 18. General Stores Transfer Account

PERFORMANCE REPORTING

Departmental performance reports can be meaningful if only direct costs are included. Even when the cost centers are fully costed with all direct and indirect costs, a separation of direct and indirect costs is useful to give unit managers information on which to base operating decisions.

For example, the supervisor on a nursing floor can possibly influence labor costs, consumption of supplies, and housekeeping services used. On the other hand, little, if any, influence can be exerted over the nursing floor's share of building depreciation, the administrator's salary, or grounds maintenance. For this reason, performance reports should sufficiently detail and break down costs to allow easy identification of that portion that can be readily controlled by the department's manager.

This chapter has discussed the identification and accumulation of costs directly incurred by individual departments. The direct costs include expenses incurred directly from within the departments, such as labor and those transferred from inventory. No mention has been made of overhead applied by straight allocation. Allocations and methods for transferring overhead and support services are discussed in detail in chapter 6.

The amount of detail reported to the department manager depends on what the manager requires and what the accounting system can provide. Generally, sufficient detail should be provided to allow the manager to measure changes in the cost of any resource used that can be independently controlled. For example, if the requirement of RNs is independent of that for ward clerks, the cost and unit cost of each should be reported as separate items in the performance reports.

The examples used in this chapter therefore show only the direct or specifically identified costs for the individual cost center.

Consider the example in table 1, below, of a monthly performance report for a nursing floor:

Table 1. Sample Monthly Performance Report for a Nursing Floor

	Actual Current month		Budget Current month		Budget variances Amount under (over) current budget
	Amount	Cost/Unit[a]	Amount	Cost/Unit	
Patient days	480		495		15
Average daily census	16		16.5		.5
Salaries and wages[b]:					
Supervisors	$ 3,675	$ 7.66	$ 3,675	$ 7.42	—
RNs	5,075	10.57	5,225	10.56	$ 150
LPNs	4,536	9.45	4,661	9.42	125
Nursing assts.	4,872	10.15	4,772	9.64	(100)
Ward clerks	1,260	2.62	1,260	2.54	—
Supplies—					
nonmedical	1,825	3.80	2,130	4.30	305
medical	3,350	6.98	3,460	6.99	110
Other direct expense	1,545	3.22	1,310	2.65	(235)
Total direct expense	$26,138	$54.45	$26,493	$53.52	$ 355

[a]Units = patient days of service
[b]Including employee benefits @ 20 percent

If this degree of detail is not needed, the report should be condensed to resemble table 2, below.

Table 2. Condensed Version of Monthly Performance Report for a Nursing Floor

	Actual Current month		Budget Current month		Budget variances Amount under (over)
	Amount	Cost/Unit	Amount	Cost/Unit	current budget
Patient days	480		495		15
Average daily census	16		16.5		.5
Salaries and wages	$19,418	$40.45	$19,593	$39.58	$ 175
Supplies	5,175	10.78	5,590	11.29	415
Other	1,545	3.22	1,310	2.65	(235)
Total direct expense	$26,138	$54.45	$26,493	$53.52	$ 355

With the number of differences apparent in the example in table 2, no clear need for the more detailed report is exhibited. Salary and wage expense per service unit are over budget because the census went down and the supervisory salary is fixed. However, there are some subtle changes that can only be determined with the more detailed report. For a three-day period, one of the nursing assistants was off sick. She was replaced with an outside agency nursing assistant, charged to the hospital at an hourly rate far higher than the hourly rate the hospital pays regular payroll nursing assistants. This is reflected in the higher nursing assistant cost for the current month as compared on budget. The supplies expense for the current month was below budget but only the detailed report shows this change.

The detail required in a performance report must be determined by each manager's needs. In addition, the use of the report must be considered. The less detailed report could be given to the director of nursing, and a one-line report (showing only totals) could go to the administrator. It is essential that reports be prepared on a timely basis and that the administrator insist that department heads explain changes. This is intended to encourage managers to become aware of the effects of their actions or lack of action and recognize the need for control. For example, if the supervisor in the examples in tables 1 and 2 knew that a change in labor cost would be noticed, she may have been more careful in substituting an agency-provided nursing assistant for the sick assistant. At the least, she should have been aware of the possible result of her decision and would have been prepared to explain the result. This is the type of control desired.

The identification of expense by responsibility center and by function or type of service rendered is also an important consideration. Responsibility cost reporting is the reporting of costs based on organizational lines and is helpful in measuring management performance. Each institution is divided into various departments under the control of different managers. Therefore, the accounting of departmental costs should be along reporting lines to facilitate the evaluation of the manager's performance.

In addition, cost centers can be subdivided by function to provide management information and to allow the computations of unit costs for services rendered. Examples include the subdivision of laboratory into the clinical and pathology section or further by type of function within these sections. Central sterile supply can be subdivided into sterile packing function and the stockroom function of inventorying medical supply handout items.

Each hospital's management should determine the level of detail that is appropriate for its needs. A breakdown of cost types (natural class, such as, labor, supplies, and so forth) within each cost center should be provided because each may require different managerial action to control. The total cost for each cost center may not provide sufficient information to assist in the day-to-day corrective actions required of management.

Alternative methods of performance reporting, on a responsibility basis with more comprehensive reports, is discussed later in this text. Even if the hospital only has a minimum performance reporting system, monthly and timely reporting of costs by department is still very useful.

CHAPTER 6

Full Costing

Chapter 5 examined techniques for recording direct expenses and explored the fundamental procedures for assigning direct expenses to appropriate cost centers. To complete the task of determining the total cost of providing patient services, known as full costing, all costs that can be directly traced to services should be charged either to the patient service cost centers or transferred to those departments through the support departments. In addition, a system should be developed to allocate the indirect overhead expense to the patient care and support cost center. The objective of this chapter is to review the following methods:

- Transferring expenses from support departments
- Allocating expenses from departments or cost centers that cannot be directly identified as applicable with patient services or support departments

In chapter 3, a basic premise is made that classifies the methods of recording expenses into three categories: direct costing, transfer costing, and allocation. Because emphasis is placed in transferring expense only on the basis of specific identification of services rendered by support departments, a transferred expense could be considered as a direct expense. For purposes of this chapter, all expenses incurred directly by a cost center or transferred in by specific identification of a support service consumed will be called *direct expense.* Overhead expense, which is allocated on some other basis, will be called *indirect expense.* The objective of the cost accounting system is to enable the hospital to minimize the use of allocations and to maximize direct costing.

The allocation of indirect costs is a necessary process in the cost accounting system. Long-range planning and establishing a responsible charge structure require management to consider all costs, both direct and indirect, that are involved in the delivery of patient services. For this reason, full costing of services is advocated.

However, full costing does not always allow for the separation of controllable and uncontrollable cost, which is essential in interim performance reporting. Therefore, an audit trail and performance measurement system should be established to report to each management level the costs directly under that respective manager's control. If hospitals were ready to establish the ideal job order system, cost control on a patient-by-patient basis could likely be achievable. In the interim, the system suggested in this and the preceding chapter allows full costing of patient services, but maintains costs for performance purposes on a responsibility basis. The presentation of the departmental cost reports is segmented to disclose direct versus indirect costs, with emphasis on avoiding arbitrary allocations whenever possible.

METHODS FOR TRANSFERRING COSTS

The selection of a method for transferring costs is important. If the manager receiving the transferred costs is to be held responsible, he should have the ability to influence the incurrence of the costs. Arbitrary step-down procedures for allocating costs may, by definition, achieve full costing; however, there is frequently little or no control over many of the allocated costs.

Generally, a cost center's service unit is the most appropriate measurement by which the costs can be transferred to the departments being serviced. Examples of commonly recognized units for transferring support service costs are:

- **Costed work orders**. Used to specifically identify and charge maintenance and repair work to departments being served
- **Time spent**. Used by service departments, such as housekeeping, the service can be based on time spent
- **Units of service delivered**. Used by departments such as the laundry, in which the service unit can be the number of pounds of laundry and linen processed

A more complete list of suggested methods of transferring costs is illustrated in figure 19, pages 48 and 49.

When developing the costs to be transferred, consideration should be given to the complexities of the services an individual support center provides. In a department rendering many different, complex services, it may not always be appropriate to divide total departmental costs by the total number of measurement units and transfer the resulting average cost to the center receiving the service. Conversely, in other departments this may be the most appropriate transfer method.

In the dietary department, for example, it may be considered appropriate to transfer all of the department's patient meal costs by using the number of equivalent patient meals served. Granted, meals served could be questioned on the basis that the special diets may be involved for some patients. However, in the long run, for accounting purposes, the production of the dietary department may be considered homogeneous. Almost all efforts and resources consumed by dietary result from a single product called patient meals served.

The maintenance department is an example of where there is more need to give recognition to the complexity of the task performed. Because each repair or renovation will likely take a different amount of effort and materials, a system should be found that allows each job to be costed to the user department according to effort required. A unit of measure that considers these complexities may be based on some type of relative value unit or detailed costed work order system.

A job cost work sheet can be used to identify and accumulate the specific materials and labor required to complete a job. Figure 20, page 50, is an example of a sample job cost work sheet. It contains spaces on which to record the individual elements of cost that are charged to a job. The costs of the materials and labor are recorded daily on the job cost work sheet as the job progresses. Material costs are determined from costed supply requisitions or from invoices. The labor costs, including employee benefits could be based on the classification of the employee performing the work or an established crew rate. In addition to the direct costs required to complete a job, a portion of the service department's overhead, both direct and indirect, should be applied to each work order and included with the job's cost. In the sample work sheet in figure 20, page 50, the overhead is applied at the rate of 25 percent of direct labor costs expended on the job. When the job is completed, these cost elements are totaled to find the cost of the job.

The total cost recorded on the job cost record is the basis for the entry that transfers the cost of the job from the maintenance department to the user department. To transfer all costs of the maintenance department to the user cost centers, a periodic (monthly) summary of all overhead allocated to maintenance will be required. Maintenance overhead would then be further allocated according to the dollar amount of work orders completed. Because the timing of the periodic transfer of overhead may not correspond to the monthly closing of the books, an estimating process, such as the one used in the example in figure 20, page 50, might be acceptable.

Employee benefits can be estimated for each employee classification to fully cost labor. Similarly, a percentage factor based on past experience could be developed for departmental overhead. These estimated factors, if used, must be checked periodically and adjusted for actual levels of expense. In order to achieve the stated goal of transferring all costs to the patient service cost centers, yet maintaining a performance record for the support departments, a transfer account can be established. This procedure is reviewed in chapter 4. Jobs in process at the end of the accounting period should also be closed and transferred to the departments receiving the service. While this should theoretically be done at the end of each month, for practical purposes it can be done at year-end closing.

The preceding example is indicative of the fact that many of the services rendered by the support departments are the completion of specific jobs for other departments. This includes central supply's preparation of packs and trays (discussed in chapter 4), housekeeping's cleaning services, and printing and duplicating services. All of these services could be costed by job work orders as previously described for the maintenance and repair department.

Another method that is often used to transfer the cost of service departments is time spent. Although time spent may be a reasonable measure of productivity, caution should be used with this method of evaluating performance. This could become an arbitrary method of allocation if time spent is inefficient, because the receiving department is charged with a proration of the serving department's costs and may not have management control over the personnel involved.

METHODS FOR ALLOCATING COSTS

Indirect Expenses Expenses that are incurred by indirect cost centers and remain undisturbed after direct transfers should also be allocated. At times, it is necessary to allocate arbitrarily because there is not a clear unit of measure over which a department manager has influence, nor is there a clear identification of the services rendered. Methods of apportioning or allocating these indirect expenses

The following list is intended for discussion purposes only. The units are only suggestions and cannot be considered as all inclusive. Each hospital must select that unit or group of units that best fits its managerial needs.

Nursing administration
1. Number of FTEs in departments supervised
2. Nursing hours of service
3. Nursing salaries of each department

Pharmacy
1. Cost of drugs, plus professional fee, by type (injectables, parenterals, tablets, or capsules)
2. Pharmacist time spent
3. Costed requisitions

Central sterile supply
1. Costed requisitions for trays and supplies
2. Relative value units times volume to each department
3. Predetermined rental rate for suction and other equipment

Social services
1. Percent of time spent
2. Number of clients, by department
3. Visit charge, by hourly rate, to departments for their clients

Medical records
1. Study charts to develop weighted statistics, by department
2. Time study of individual positions
3. Percent of time spent, by patient floor

General stores
1. Requisition charge, materials and storage charge "costed requisitions"
2. Spoilage should be charged back to using departments

Interns and residents
1. Assigned time
2. Time spent
3. Hourly charge for private physicians' inpatient emergencies and other hospital calls

Laundry and linen
1. Pounds of laundry
2. Pieces of linen, per piece charge
3. Pounds of laundry, weighted by pressed or nonpressed
4. Allocate linen replacement costs to departments

Housekeeping
1. Hours of service
2. Weighted square feet, by type of area
3. Charge all cleaning supplies directly to departments, then charge time and equipment costs
4. Charge basic care by weighted square feet, add in charges for nonroutine service based on time, equipment, supplies, and overhead

Dietary and cafeteria
1. Meals served
2. Weighted meals, by special diet
3. Weighted meals, by floor served

Figure 19. Methods of Transferring Costs

4. Sales value of meals, by department
5. By component of service:
   a. Therapeutic Dietician, time spent
   b. Dietary: weighted meals, by floor
   c. Cafeteria, dollar value of meals served

Maintenance and repairs
1. Departmental square feet
2. Costed work requisitions
3. Square feet for routine work, covered requisitions for special projects
4. All outside service costs "passed through" to departments

Security
1. Areas patrolled
2. Number of incidents, by area

Operation of plant
1. Departmental square feet
2. Utility costs:
   a. Engineering study of actual usage
   b. Metered consumption
3. Square feet, weighted by weekly hours of operation

Depreciation—Movable equipment
1. Dollar value by department
2. Actual departmental depreciation based on detailed equipment records

Employee health and welfare
1. Gross salaries
2. Individual components may be distributed on the following bases:
   a. FICA expense:
      • FICA withholding by department
      • FICA salaries by department
   b. Hospitalization insurance:
      • Departmental analysis of premium expense
      • Number of employees insured by department
   c. Disability insurance
      • Number of employees insured by department
      • Departmental covered (insured) salaries
   d. Group life insurance
      • Departmental insurable salaries
   e. Pension costs
      • Direct to departments on basis of cost data prepared by actuary on individual basis
   f. Workmen's compensation
      • Department-covered salaries
   g. Personnel department expenses
      • Number of employees interviewed by department
   h. Employee health services
      • Number of employees examined by department
3. Holiday and vacation pay should be loaded directly into the labor cost department by department and recorded as earned not as taken.
4. All of the employee benefits can be payroll-loaded and charged directly to the departments with the payroll. This is easier under a standard rather than actual system.

Figure 19 (continued)

Job Cost Work Sheet					
Department being served Emergency Medicine Department Job no. 8-14					
Description of job Paint complete department					
Date job to start ____ 8/07/XX ____ Est. completion date ____ 8/10/XX					
Actual completion date ____ 8/09/XX ____ Job supervisor ___ R. Chambers					
Personnel assigned to job _____ L. Fedders and J. Fuller					

Costs Incurred					
Labor used					
Date	Employee name	Employee ID no.	Hours charged	Hourly labor rate	Total cost
8/07/XX	Fedders	369-5	8	4.93	$ 39.44
8/07/XX	Fuller	490-5	4	4.93	19.72
8/08/XX	Chambers	510-4	4	5.53	22.12
8/08/XX	Fuller	490-5	4	4.93	19.72
8/09/XX	Fuller	490-5	8	4.93	39.44
Total Labor Cost			28	5.02	$140.44
Materials used					
Date	Supply requisition or PD no.	Description of materials	Units used	Unit cost	Total cost
*8/07/XX	8-499	Paint, green	13 gal.	$4.95	$ 65.35
*8/08/XX	8-693	Paint, green	5 gal.	4.95	24.75
Total Materials Cost					$ 89.10
Service center overhead applied					34.43
Total Job Costs					$263.97

*An alternative method of recording the use of materials could be to have the department receiving the service requisition the materials directly.

Figure 20. Sample Job Cost Work Sheet: Maintenance and Repair Services

on hospitals include such measures as:
- Patient days
- Square feet
- Accumulated costs
- Total costs of all departments

Careful analysis of the allocation base is required because of the danger of distortion. If the costs of patient accounting, admitting, and registration were allocated on the basis of patient days, only the cost centers that have patient days would absorb these expenses. True distribution of these services would require the use of an equivalent to patient days for outpatient services and the number of admissions per department. Also the use of square feet to allocate depreciation, taxes, and energy costs can distort because the mere existence of footage may not relate to the cost of the structure or of energy used.

Each hospital should review the nature of expenses incurred by each indirect overhead department. The review should be made at the lowest level of responsibility and maintained with the objective of identifying a unit of measure that could be used to allocate costs on a fair basis to user departments.

Examples of indirect expenses influenced by other department managers and some methods used for apportionment are:

- **Personnel Department.** Number of employees assigned to or salaries in each cost center
- **Data Processing Department.** Central processing units (CPU) spent, print time, or the number of inquiries for each department served, with actual charges of labor, CPU time, and overhead for special programs developed
- **Purchasing Department.** Number of purchase orders processed or dollars of purchases
- **Communications Cost Center.** Number of nonpatient phones in each department or actual charges by phone, separate charges for patient phones

Note that the unit of productivity used to measure performance of a cost center may, at times, not be the best measure for transferring or allocating the costs to user departments. These examples demonstrate the possibility of separate measures for departmental performance and the transfer of costs. The number of employees throughout the hospital may be the only measure available by which to allocate undistributed personnel department costs, but may not relate to the efficient operation of the department. Figure 21, next page, includes a more detailed set of examples of methods to apportion indirect overhead expenses.

Indirect expenses should be apportioned and transferred to the other cost centers on a periodic basis. Each cost center should be assigned one or more natural expense classifications to which the overhead is charged. The level of detail considered appropriate should be determined by each hospital. Each indirect overhead center should credit an overhead applied account (transfer account) to transfer its total period costs to the patient care and support cost centers. This is explained in chapter 4 in the purchasing and stores example. An automated system could make the transfer a normal procedure in the monthly closing process.

If apportioned overhead is reflected on departmental financial cost reports, it should be shown separately from the direct expenses over which the manager has control. This separation provides a more responsible measure of the productivity of the individual manager by allowing a focus on expenses under the manager's control versus those that are allocated on an arbitrary basis.

By-products   In a production shop in which by-products are produced as a normal part of the manufacturing process, the by-product is not assigned a pro rata portion of overhead. The minor revenue received from the by-product is recorded as a reduction in the cost of producing the major product or treated as miscellaneous income. There may be a similar situation in hospitals. Some activities that are not a part of the hospital's formal purpose, such as recovery of silver in the radiology department or the sale of placentas, should not be considered as a separate function or bear a pro rata share of indirect overhead. An appropriate treatment would be to consider these special activities as a marginal activity that is charged only with specific direct costs. The resulting net revenue would be considered as a recovery of the direct costs incurred to carry on these activities, with any excess of revenue resulting from the direct

Methods of Allocating Costs

This list is for discussion only and is not all-inclusive. Each hospital must make a decision on allocations on the basis of each manager's needs. Allocations should be kept to a minimum. Direct costing and specific identification are more acceptable methods of assuming costs.

Personnel
1. Number of FTEs or hours worked
2. Base charge for number of FTEs, plus charges for new lines and counseling time, by department
3. Pass through costs of employment agency and advertising costs

Communications
1. Number of telephone lines or instruments
2. By component:
   a. Number of nonpatient lines
   b. Number of patient lines
   c. Additional communication services (answering service, executive, intercom, piped-in music)—weighted service charge
3. By actual charges at each station

Utilization review
1. Number of cases reviewed, by inpatient department

Data processing
1. Machine time
2. CPU time
3. Number of cards punched or print time
4. Number of inquiries

Admitting and patient accounts
1. Gross charges, by department
2. Average daily census, by department
3. Number of admissions, transfers and discharges by department
4. Weighted units for admissions and outpatient registrations

Insurance
1. Professional liability insurance on same basis as premium was computed: beds, visit, or dollars of exposure as calculated by carrier
2. Fire insurance based on appraised value of each building and departmental square feet
3. Property insurance based on square feet

Administrative and general
1. Number of inpatient days, plus a percentage of expenses allocated to outpatient and ancillary departments
2. Number of FTEs
3. Accumulated costs, by departments

Purchasing
1. Number of special requisitions, by department
2. Number of stock items, by department
3. Dollar volume of purchases, by department

Figure 21. Methods of Allocating Costs

cost of performing the activity considered a reduction in the operating expense of radiology and delivery, respectively.

ACCOUNTING SYSTEM'S INVOLVEMENT IN TRANSFERRING COSTS

The cost accounting system should provide for the accumulation of the units of support services delivered. At the end of each reporting period, the system should automatically transfer the costs of rendering the services to the user departments. Actual costs of the service department can be averaged over the number of services rendered. This average cost for each service unit is transferred to the receiving departments.

The cost transfers should be done by using a series of transfer accounts in the general ledger as described in chapter 5. The transfer account serves as a revenue account for the service department, and the detail of its costs remain intact. (The transfer accounts are also referred to as reciprocal accounts or cost application accounts.) The direct costs of a cost center would be recorded by their natural classification, such as salaries and benefits, supplies, purchased services, and so forth. This detail would be maintained for the department in the general ledger. The transfer account would be established in the general ledger to record the cost of services provided to other cost centers.

For example, statement of costs for the laundry and linen department could present the information illustrated in table 3, next page. In table 3, the total costs incurred by the laundry and linen cost center are transferred to the user cost centers. Average costs must be computed and transferred monthly unless cost standards are developed. The monthly average will vary with the efficiency of the department.

PERFORMANCE REPORTS RESULTING FROM THE COST ACCOUNTING SYSTEM

Chapter 5 discusses the identification and accumulation of costs incurred directly by individual departments and how cost reports can be meaningful only if direct costs are included. In this chapter, the discussion concerns the transfer of costs from the support service cost centers and the apportionment of expenses from the indirect overhead, general and administrative cost centers. An example of these costs added to the performance reports presented in chapter 5 follows. As stated in chapter 5, a separation of direct and indirect costs is useful to give unit managers information on which to base operating decisions. This concept is continued in the example in table 4, page 55. If this degree of detail is not needed, the report could be condensed to the example in table 5, page 56.

The department manager can now determine the costs involved in using services from a support department and, to some extent, control costs for these services. Although the department manager may not gain complete control over the support service expenses, he at least knows what his share is and may be able to affect some influence over these costs. The indirect expenses are uncontrollable at this management level.

Table 3. Laundry Department Monthly Cost Statement

		Unit costs[a]
Costs incurred		
Salaries and wages	$ 3,685.00	$ 6.70
Employee benefits	665.50	1.21
Purchased laundry and linen services	6,050.00	11.00
Departmental supplies	566.50	1.03
Total direct costs	10,967.00	19.94
Support service costs transferred in:		
Housekeeping services	786.50	1.43
Maintenance and repairs	313.50	0.57
Total support costs	1,100.00	2.00
Allocated indirect overhead	1,573.00	2.86
Total departmental costs	$13,640.00	$24.80
Costs transferred to using cost centers		
Nursing units (41,800 lb.)	$10,366.40	
Nursery unit (3,850 lb.)	954.80	
Labor and delivery room (2,200 lb.)	545.60	
Operating room (7,150 lb.)	1,773.20	
Total costs transferred	$13,640,00	
Total dry and clean pounds processed	55,000 lbs.	
Total average cost per 100 lb. processed	$24.80	

[a]Per 100 lb. laundry processed.

Table 4. Sample Monthly Performance Report with Direct and Support Expenses

	Actual Current month		Budget Current month		Budget variances Amount under (over) current budget
	Amount	Cost/Unit[a]	Amount	Cost/Unit	
Service units:					
Patient days	480		495		15
Average daily census	16		16.5		.5
Direct expenses:					
Salaries and wages:					
Supervisors	$ 3,675	$ 7.66	$ 3,675	$ 7.42	—
RNs	5,075	10.57	5,225	10.56	$ 150
LPNs	4,536	9.45	4,661	9.42	125
Nursing assts.	4,872	10.15	4,772	9.64	(100)
Ward clerks	1,260	2.62	1,260	2.54	—
Supplies—					
nonmedical	1,825	3.80	2,130	4.30	305
medical	3,350	6.98	3,460	6.99	110
Other direct expense	1,545	3.22	1,310	2.65	(235)
Total direct expenses	26,138	54.45	26,493	53.52	355
Support expenses (transferred):					
Housekeeping	2,760	5.75	2,920	5.90	160
Laundry and linen	2,275	4.74	2,435	4.92	160
Maintenance and repairs	2,120	4.42	1,870	3.78	(250)
Dietary	5,325	11.09	5,492	11.09	167
Total transferred expenses	12,480	26.00	12,717	25.69	237
Support expenses (allocated):					
Administrative and general	3,312	6.90	3,416	6.90	104
Personnel	925	1.93	1,073	2.17	148
Total allocated expenses	4,237	8.83	4,489	9.07	252
Total department expenses	$42,855		$43,699		$844
Per patient day		$89.28		$88.28	

[a]Unit = Per patient day. Patient days are used only for illustrative purposes. Other more sophisticated statistics may be developed and used in the appropriate instances.

Table 5. Condensed Monthly Performance Report with Direct and Support Expenses

	Actual Current month		Budget Current month		Budget variances Amount under (over) current budget
	Amount	Cost/Unit	Amount	Cost/Unit	
Service units:					
Patient days	480		495		15
Average daily census	16		16.5		.5
Direct expenses:					
Salaries and wages	$19,418	$40.45	$19,593	$39.58	$ 175
Supplies	5,175	10.78	5,590	11.29	415
Other	1,545	3.22	1,310	2.65	(235)
Total direct expenses	26,138	54.45	26,493	53.52	355
Support expenses (transferred)	12,480	26.00	12,717	25.69	237
Support expenses (allocated)	4,237	8.83	4,489	9.07	252
Total department expenses	$42,855		$43,699		$ 844
Per patient day		$89.28		$88.28	

CHAPTER 7

Cost Analysis in Decision Making

The purpose of cost accounting is to assist managers in controlling costs by providing them with pertinent information on cost behavior. To emphasize which costs should be evaluated when managers make operating decisions, this chapter develops new perspectives on the cost information presented thus far. First, there is a brief discussion of two alternative costing methods: full costing and direct costing. Following this, the key concept of relevant costs is presented, with several operating examples. The final section addresses cost analysis for capital equipment decisions and special service decisions. The objective of this chapter is to provide managers with a sound basis for determining the best use of cost data and the most appropriate cost-reporting format for making their decisions.

In the preceding chapters, a basic cost information system was presented. The full cost of providing care was shown to include three types of costs:

- Costs incurred directly by a cost center
- Costs transferred from support cost centers to patient service cost centers
- General and administrative overhead allocated to patient care and support service cost centers

The basic cost information system is structured to assist managers with assessing department productivity and to provide supervisors with measurement tools and key indicators to help pinpoint problem areas and improve departmental performance. The system is geared to providing information on the ongoing, long-term operations of the hospital. This presentation of costs includes relevant direct, transferred, and allocated costs in the decision-making process. Full or absorption costing can be used in special project analysis.

Another method of presenting costs when analyzing operations can be germane to evaluating cost reduction programs, capital equipment decisions, special services, or pricing policy. This method is marginal costing (also known as variable or direct costing). The objective of direct costing is to compare the cash outflow (direct costs, including transferred costs, of the equipment or changes in services) with the inflow (earnings or savings resulting from the equipment or changes). Advocates of this method are of the opinion that the full-costing method clouds the decision-making process by including many costs that might be irrelevant to the issue at hand. For example, the allocation of existing indirect costs to a new service will overstate the incremental costs of providing the service.

It is not the purpose of this text to advocate either full costing or direct costing. Both methods will be given, and the manager should choose the method most appropriate for his own situation.

RELEVANT COSTS

Hospital management is required to make an increasing number of complex operating decisions. These decisions require the consideration of many relevant factors, only a few of which are easily quantified. Management must assess each operating decision in light of:

- The community's needs
- The regulatory environment
- Third-party pressures
- Quality of care
- The effort to maximize the benefits resulting from an expenditure of resources

A simple description of relevant costs for a particular decision process is: the cost relevant to a particular decision is only the cost that will differ between the alternatives being considered.

The process of determining relevant costs is often problematic. In some cases, it is not possible to compute or identify the actual cost difference between alternatives. The most efficacious manner in which to develop this concept is to present two operating decisions and detail the reasoning process that is used to arrive at the costs that are relevant to each decision. The following examples reflect the determination of relevant costs in two operating decisions.

Table 6, below, presents an example of nursing floor costs. First, consider the decision of staff composition on a nursing unit. With either method of cost presentation, the only relevant financial data may be the cost differential between RNs, LPNs, nursing assistants, ward clerks, and so forth. The impact on quality of care would be weighed against the cost of replacing a nursing assistant with an LPN or reducing RN time spent on administrative duties by replacing an aide with a unit manager. Note that, in this situation, the costs are easily identified. They are, for the most part, variable with the service units.

Table 6. Nursing Floor Costs Report

Direct expenses:	Month of May
Supervisor salaries	$ 2,500
RNs	8,100
LPNs	4,400
Nursing assts.	3,400
Supplies	2,600
Leases	950
Support expenses (transferred):	
Housekeeping	1,800
Maintenance and repairs	1,200
Miscellaneous	650
Support expense (allocated):	
Depreciation	3,500
	$29,100

Consider a more difficult situation. The nursing floor in question has 25 beds, most of which are semiprivate, with an average charge of $58 per day. The average ancillary charges per patient day total $22. The administrator of the hospital wants to evaluate removal of four beds from service and making offices out of the two rooms involved.

The controller gathers the following data for consideration in the decision:
- The average daily census of the floor has been 20 patients.
- There were 65 days during the past year when the census was above 21 patients. The average daily census during that period was 23 patients.
- If the floor is cut to 21 beds, the staff can be cut by one RN at $1,350 per month, one LPN at $1,100 per month, and one assistant at $800 per month.
- Building depreciation of $3,500 per month is allocated to the floor on the basis of $140 per month per bed.
- The supervisors' salaries of $2,500 per month will stay the same.
- Housekeeping service will be cut as the reassigned space will not require the same degree of service, as it will be offices rather than patient rooms.
- The occupancy of the unit has remained nearly constant over the past 5 years and is expected to remain constant in the near future.

What costs are relevant to the administrator's decision? Consider each of the elements just listed and other data from the montly cost summary for the floor.
- Supervisors' salaries will remain fixed under either alternative and are therefore irrelevant.
- Total salaries cost will change. The estimated savings of $3,250 per month is relevant.
- Supplies expense is a variable cost. It will be relevant only if the number of patients served is altered by the decision.
- Depreciation will change by shifting the allocation for the two rooms from the nursing floor and to the offices. Total depreciation is a factor of the original cost of the building and thus is a sunk cost. For the hospital, depreciation does not change under either decision and is not relevant.
- Maintenance is charged to the floor on a job order basis and will not be altered by the decision to close two rooms. Any cost associated with preparing the two rooms for use as office space is relevant.
- Leases are relevant only if an equipment lease is terminated.
- Housekeeping is charged on the basis of time spent. The housekeeping allocation for the two rooms will be shifted, in a reduced amount, to the offices. This is not relevant to the decision because the decreased workload will not result in a reduction of the hospital's housekeeping staff.

Management must also evaluate the revenue implications of the decision. Will there be any revenue lost? It is probable that, for 65 days a year, two of the four beds taken out of service would be needed. This could be stated as:

65 days @ 2 beds @ $80 per bed day = $10,400 lost revenue per year
$10,400 ÷ 12 = $867 lost revenue per month

However, this revenue lost is relevant only if patients are turned away. If they will be transferred to different floors, the revenue loss is not relevant to the decision.

The administrator can make his decision by using the following relevant information:

- There could be a revenue loss of $867 per month, which may be avoided by using beds on other floors.
- Salaries will decrease $3,250 per month.
- No fixed cost is added to the other departments.

If the quality of care on the floor is not affected, the administrator will likely proceed with his plan to convert two of the rooms to office space.

In making that decision, note that knowledge of the variable or fixed nature of the cost and revenue implications is helpful. This can be true for any operating decision, because the fixed costs are sunk and committed, whereas the variable costs can be influenced or altered. For this reason, consider restating the nursing floor's May performance costs report in the format illustrated in table 7, below.

Table 7. Nursing Floor Report Including Variable Costs

	Month of May
Patient revenue—600 patient days	$48,000
Less variable expense:	
Variable labor:	
RNs (1.8 FTEs variable RN labor)	2,430
LPNs	2,200
Nursing assts.	1,700
Supplies	2,600
Housekeeping	800
Maintenance and repairs	1,200
Total variable expense	10,930
Contribution margin after variable expense	37,070
Less fixed expense:	
Fixed portion of labor:	
Supervisors' salary	2,500
RNs (4.2 FTEs fixed RN labor)	5,670
LPNs	2,200
Nursing assts.	1,700
Leases	950
Housekeeping	1,000
Miscellaneous	650
Total fixed expense	14,670
Contribution margin after variable and fixed expense	22,400
Less depreciation:	3,500
Contribution margin before general and administrative overhead	$18,900

To prepare the monthly report in the manner prescribed in table 7 requires an analysis of each cost element to determine the fixed and variable nature of each. If done accurately, the department manager has cost information classified by degree of control or flexibility. For the most part, short-term operating changes will affect only variable expenses and revenues. As such, marginal costing may be the most appropriate method.

A full costing system allocates other costs, such as dietary, pharmacy, central sterile supply, and general and administrative overhead. For day-to-day operating decisions, the allocation of costs such as general and administrative overhead or depreciation may be of limited usefulness because of the irrelevant nature of these costs in short-term decisions. However, there may be some usefulness in demonstrating to the department head the amount of contribution margin necessary to operate the entire hospital. The decision as to the degree of detail reported must be made on the basis of individual hospital policy. However, each department head must be educated in the determination of relevant versus irrelevant cost data for decision making. Departmental reporting on a direct costing basis, as in table 7, page 60, can be helpful, as the cost breakdown more closely depicts the relationship of cost to volume.

CAPITAL EQUIPMENT DECISIONS

Capital expenditure decisions require a somewhat different analysis. The rule for the determination of relevant costs is unchanged. However, relevant costs will differ because of the longer time span affected by the decision. Some costs are always irrelevant:

- The original cost and present book value of old equipment that is to be discarded
- Depreciation expense related to the old equipment and the proposed new equipment

Capital expenditure decisions require the analysis of incremental costs associated with the expenditure and the revenue considerations that may either differ as a result of the new equipment or will be produced by added services.

Assume that a hospital has extra space in its radiology department and its radiologists have asked for a special procedures room, equipped for their use in treating patients now being treated in other hospitals. As this is a new service with new equipment, many predictions are required, each based on the best judgment of management. The prediction exercise may require discussions with management of other hospitals to learn their experience. Predictions required include:

- The revenue to be generated by the special procedures room and the related expenses
- Increase in patient census and resulting increase in other patient revenue and operating expenses
- Professional fees to be paid the radiologists
- Impact on expenses that would otherwise have remained fixed
- Useful life and salvage value of the equipment being purchased

Assume that, without the special procedures room, the radiology department's statement of operating results is as illustrated in table 8, next page.

Table 8. Radiology Department Operating Results without Special Procedures Room

	Per procedure	Total
Patient revenue (150,000 procedures)	$10.00	$1,500,000
Variable expenses:		
Professional fees (30%)	3.00	450,000
Labor and materials	3.00	450,000
Total variable expenses	6.00	900,000
Contribution margin	4.00	600,000
Fixed expenses:		
Departmental	1.33	200,000
Support services	0.67	100,000
General overhead	0.67	100,000
Total fixed expenses	2.67	400,000
Excess of revenues over expenses	$ 1.33	$ 200,000

Using the rule of relevance stated earlier, the following analysis is necessary to consider the financial implications of this decision.
- The fixed expenses of operating the radiology department will not change. The present $400,000 total of fixed expenses is not relevant.
- The radiologist estimates that 20,000 procedures will be performed by the new special procedures room per year, at a net revenue of $8 each. As incremental revenue, it is relevant to the decision.
- The operation of the new room will cost $2.40 per procedure for the radiologist fees (30 percent of net revenue), with labor and material costing $3.00 per procedure. At the predicted volume, the contribution margin from the new procedures will be $2.60 per procedure, as opposed to $4.00 per procedure for the present radiology exams.
- The new room will cost $200,000 to prepare and equip, will have a useful life of ten years, and will have only a nominal salvage value at that time.
- The radiologist thinks that his colleagues will be admitting new patients as a result of the new services, thus increasing the census by three patients per day. The additional revenue from these patients, less the variable costs associated with their hospital stay, is relevant to the decision.

A brief analysis of the relevant cost data is given in table 9, next page.

Table 9. Special Procedures Room Relevant Cost Data

Additional revenue per year, 20,000 @ $8	=	$160,000
Additional cost per year:		
Professional fees, 20,000 @ $2.40	=	48,000
Labor and materials, 20,000 @ 3.00	=	60,000
		108,000
Additional contribution margin in radiology department		$ 52,000

At this point in the analysis, the conclusion is that the hospital will likely receive at least $52,000 more per year for the next ten years for an initial $200,000 investment. In addition, the net increase in cash flow from the added inpatient load of three patients per day should be considered. Other factors that should be gathered before making a final decision might be maintenance costs on the new room in future years, a cost analysis of the option to lease the equipment, added utility costs, and the probability of obsolescence of the equipment as a result of technological changes in the next ten years.

In this example, the $52,000 per year in added cash flow will likely lead to a decision to equip the new special procedures room. The initial investment of $200,000 will be recovered by the additional cash flow within the radiology department without considering the likelihood of additional inpatient revenue. Although the additional inpatient revenue is relevant, care should be taken in using this as part of the decision process because the radiologist's estimate of what his associates will do on an inpatient basis may be very speculative.

Note that it is not necessary for the depreciation expense for the new equipment to be considered as an added expense. The depreciation expense would be the systematic amortization of the original cost ($200,000) over the life of the new special procedures room. This has already been considered in the $200,000 original investment.

To properly relate the net increase in the cash flow for the next ten years, a discounted cash flow analysis should be applied to the future cash flows to bring all cost considerations to a common present value level. This will allow the comparision of future cash flows (years 1 through 10) with the $200,000 investment to be made at the outset. This may also be necessary if the $200,000 investment is based on financing that spreads the payment of the initial investment over the next several years. Discounted cash flow analysis is not discussed in this text. However, a good controller will always add this useful tool to his capital budgeting process.

SPECIAL TREATMENT FOR SPECIAL UNITS OR SERVICES

In the health care environment, new services will continue to be added that are possibly not perceived as part of a normal hospital service today. In addition, hospitals might become involved with a countless number of projects outside their original purpose. These could include meals on wheels, outreach clinics or ambulatory care centers, medical office buildings, long-term care facilities, or other community involvement projects. If projects of this kind are considered, the cost implications will need special consideration. This will ensure that the cost accounting system, originally intended to account only for the main hospital structure and operation, is not distorted by the unusual nature of the new service.

Consider an example such as a remote outreach clinic operated by the hospital as a community service. If, when making the initial decision to lease and operate the clinic, the hospital's management had analyzed and considered a full costing of the clinic's services including full allocation of all hospital overhead, the cost of the clinic would be overstated. At the very least, many of the overhead costs applied would have violated the rule of relevance stated in this chapter. If the full-costed clinic services were part of the decisions to proceed, charges determined necessary to justify the project might be higher than can be reasonably charged, and a community service might be lost.

Using the marginal or incremental costing techniques described in this chapter, the decision process used to determine the financial appropriateness of the clinic would only include the following:

- Revenue expected to be received by the new clinic
- Incremental outlays to lease or purchase the clinic
- Marginal increases in costs by the main hospital to provide support for the new facility
- The direct cost of operating the new clinic

Defending the marginal or incremental process in the decision to proceed with the clinic is easily done on the basis of concepts described in this chapter. However, there is still another question. After operation of the clinic is underway, should the cost accounting system described in the preceding chapters be implemented into the clinic operation as if it were an integrated part of the main hospital? A strong case can be made to support special treatment of the services that are not part of the hospital's primary purpose. Consider the following reasons for not fully costing special services:

- Full costing would overstate the cost of the clinic and understate the cost of operating the main hospital by relieving the main hospital of overhead burden that would have occurred despite the existence of the clinic.
- Full costing would eventually result in higher prices for needed community clinical services and underpricing of the main hospital services.
- If the clinic operation were closed at a future date, only the direct costs of the clinic would be eliminated. The original overhead burden would fall back on the main hospital, which had adjusted rates inappropriately and therefore may have been underpricing its service.
- Any cost accounting system that uses arbitrary allocations to cost a particular service runs the danger of destroying the usefulness of the performance measurements system.

If new services are proposed with full consideration of the community services involved, proper evaluation of financial efficiency and appropriateness might not be served by full costing but rather by marginal costing that service. This can be true for services added to an acute hospital such as long-term care units, medical office buildings, and special treatment units for such care as hemodialysis. Care should be taken when considering an accounting process that may comply with an accounting or regulatory principle at the expense of good judgment based on sound, relevant cost implications.

In summary, one responsibility of a cost accounting system is to provide managers with relevant data that will lead them toward the optimal decision when evaluating several options. A working knowlege of the contribution margin approach to cost analysis and the ability to distinguish between relevant and irrelevant factors are basic to many decisions. The objective is to compare those factors that are different among alternatives. Essential to the effective use of a cost accounting system is the ability to decide which data and format are most informative for the decision at hand.

SECTION III. COST ACCOUNTING SYSTEM

CHAPTER **8**

Standard Costs

The basic cost information system discussed in section II, chapters 3 through 7, is limited in its ability to provide the information necessary for several key management reports. As discussed in chapter 3, the ideal cost accounting system is one with standards. The enhancements that should be included in such a system are discussed in this chapter and in chapters 9 through 11. The most fundamental of these system enhancements is the development and use of standard costs. The use of standards for cost accounting and performance measurement is fairly common in American industry. Yet, in hospitals, the use of standard costs is rare. This might indicate either that hospitals are missing a valuable tool or that the complexities of the health care industry are such that standard costs are too difficult to implement. In reality, the implementation of standard costing in hospitals is a difficult and complex task. However, the potential rewards are significant. The purpose of this section is to present the fundamentals of standard costing for hospitals and outline the principal ways in which such a system can be used.

Standard costs are the basis for budgeting and performance reporting. They are, in effect, established objectives that should be attained or achieved by an efficient operation. Standard costs are used to measure efficiency. Efficiency can be measured by ascertaining the number of inputs (resources consumed) required to produce outputs (services rendered). Effectiveness, on the other hand, has long been a prime health care objective. Effectiveness is a measure of the delivery of health care service or, in other words, its accomplishment. Standards can, of course, be used to measure both, but principally they are used to assist hospital management in the measurement of efficiency.

There are standards to determine the appropriate usage of labor, supplies, and other resources required by a cost center to provide service units. The term *standard* is not intended to mean the same as a budget. Budget determination is the appropriate total usage on an aggregate basis. A standard can be defined as the budget for a single unit and can be stated in units of resource input per unit of service or of cost, or both. Standards provide the basis for measuring performance and developing meaningful budgets, as well as providing a necessary tool to make evaluations and render proper decisions.

The development and implementation of a standard cost system encourages a managerial attitude and provides an information base that is very beneficial, specifically:

- **Organizational improvements.** Improved organizational definition can be a natural outgrowth of setting standards. If standards are properly utilized for control purposes, they are determined on the basis of cost responsibility. If lines of authority and responsibility are not clearly delineated in the organization, the deficiencies will be exposed in the process of initiating the standard cost system.

- **Understanding the nature and behavior of costs.** This understanding is developed in the process of setting standards. The fixed and variable nature of each expense element must be investigated as part of the process. Comparison of actual costs with standard costs and investigation of the causes of variance provide insight into cost behavior.

- **Proper pricing of existing and contemplated services.** Without the presence of standard costs, many hospitals practice a flat-rate billing system for room and board; furthermore, this rate is established with only limited knowledge of the costs of component services included in the room rate. Prices for ancillary services are often based on the charges of competing hospitals or third-party price limitations. Standard costs will establish for existing and new services a pricing mechanism based on more complete knowledge of the cost implications of providing the services.

- **Measurement of operating performance.** From a management standpoint, actual costs are not as significant as the variance of actual from standard costs. Through the timely reporting of these variances, management can ascertain whether opportunities exist for short-range cost reduction or long-range cost containment exercises. This is even more appropriate in hospitals, in which labor costs are a substantial portion of total cost. The magnitude of human resource expenditures in any hospital demands an economic, effective system of allocating manpower that is sufficiently flexible to accommodate changing patient needs. To be effective, the manpower allocation system must be accurate, timely, and able to provide a measure of productivity and a framework for cost containment. The standard cost system responds precisely to these criteria.

- **Computation and transfer of unit costs for support services is simplified.** The cost information system, as presented in section II, requires the periodic computation of the cost of service units. The use of standards for transferring support services will eliminate the need for this computation prior to transfer. This will facilitate periodic entries to record transfers and allocations. Actual unit costs can be determined later and analyzed as part of the variance analysis.

STANDARDS FOR DIRECT EXPENSE

In an ideal setting, standards are set by industrial engineers, with the accounting department providing the necessary information to apply a unit cost to the standards. In a practical sense, standards are set by using a combination of historical information, work studies, and engineering technology. Also, it is essential that a system be established to monitor and maintain the standards on a current basis. The standards should always be relevant to current cost behavior patterns if they are to be fair and attainable. Thus, they will be useful to management as a measurement tool. Standards should be tight and demand a high degree of efficiency. However, if they are unattainable or unrealistic, the department manager might have no more motivation to increase efficiency than he would have without the standards.

Standard costs can be categorized into standards for the measurement of direct expenses, transferred expenses, and allocated or overhead expenses. The measurement of the variances from standard depends on the nature of the type of expense under consideration. For example, direct expenses, such as material costs, are affected by two primary factors: price and quantity. Material price standards can be based on anticipated prices for the time frame in question (normally, a year) or on prices prevailing at the time the standards are established. The purchasing officer of the hospital should have a strong role in setting price standards.

Standard quantities of material per unit of product, including unavoidable waste, can be ascertained through several techniques. Estimates by department personnel, statistical analyses of historical data, and engineering studies can be utilized to determine the usage of material. In a health care environment, a high degree of accuracy for material usage and total cost may not be necessary in most departments, as the dollar amounts, compared with labor, are relatively small. The standard quantity of material required per unit of product, multiplied by the standard price per unit of that material, is the standard cost for that material. Deviation of actual cost from this standard should be analyzed to determine how much is a result of usage variation and how much is a result of price variation.

In a similar manner, standards for other nonlabor expenses can be developed. These standards should reflect the usage and price per unit of output, if such information is available or if it can be determined through various management engineering techniques. Some areas in which the development of usage standards is appropriate are:

- Payroll-related employee benefits
- Nonpayroll-related employee benefits
- Medical professional fees
- Certain services purchased by volume (for example, hours per month of security service or CPU of prime time from the computer service bureau)
- Utilities

For other types of direct or transferred nonlabor expenses, standards can be developed through direct identification of cost. This method is also appropriate in the areas just listed, in which the cost to develop and maintain usage standards may be prohibitive. Standards for expenses such as interest, depreciation, property taxes, licenses, and so forth can be set at a periodic fixed level or through an estimate of the desired level of expenditure in relation to planned volume of service (for example, professional membership dues, subscriptions, purchased services, and so forth). It is better to have a standard that measures responsibility by specific identification of a fixed charge per time period or that relates to volume of specific services used than to allocate the expense on some arbitrary basis.

Establishing standards for direct expenses, such as labor cost, is a procedure closely analogous to that of setting material cost standards; however, the methodologies differ markedly. Acceptable methods of work measurement range from simple, such as historical data gathering, to complicated, such as the application of management science techniques. Each methodology has its advantages and disadvantages as well as its individual adaptability to specific hospital departments, depending on the existing data available and the work to be measured.

Because physical units of measurement are not always developed for human work, the work measurement practitioner may be obliged to measure effort somewhat subjectively. Observed effort is rated in comparison with a conceptualization of "normal effort." The rating is expressed as a percentage of observed effort. This aspect of work measurement relies heavily on specialized skills of a trained practitioner, such as a management engineer. The product of rated effort and observed time is called normal time and represents work content. Thus, the normal time established for a particular task corresponds to the time required to perform one cycle of that task by a person working at the normal level of effort.

Because of fatigue resulting from repeated performances of the task, the necessity of interrupting work, and certain other factors contributing to an unavoidable diminution in productivity, allowances are added to work content. This enables determination of a standard time that can reasonably be met by a properly trained and supervised worker over an extended period of time.

The key to measuring work is in the identification of objective, tangible evidence of productive efforts. These quantifiable work units can include the following:

Department	Work unit activities
Food service	Patient meals, cafeteria meals
Laundry	Pounds, pieces
Housekeeping	Square footage or weighted square footage
Laboratory	Number of tests or relative value units
Radiology	Number of exams or relative value units
Nursing service	Hours per patient day

In order to develop labor standards, the specific procedures and set of conditions in the work place must be well defined so that the appropriate measurement can be made. Furthermore, a system must be in use to record and report the quantifiable work units produced according to the specific procedures and set of conditions measured.

Conventional work measurement consists of five basic steps:
- Recording the method
- Timing of elements
- Rating of effort
- Calculating normal time
- Determining standard time

Assume that the chemistry laboratory is a typical pathology cost center in which a labor standard is to be developed. The following procedure illustrates the labor standard for a technologist to perform the necessary work to process a specific chemistry procedure.

Method	Timing	×	Rating =	Normal Time
Work element	**Observed hours** **100 tests**			
Instructions	2.50		80%	2.000
Review procedures	0.50		100%	0.500
Prepare solutions/reagents	1.00		80%	0.800
Process specimen	4.00		125%	5.000
Miscellaneous clerical	0.50		100%	0.500

Normal time per 100 chemistry procedures = 8.800

Normal time + Allowances = Standard time/100 chemistry procedures

8.800 + 15% (8.800) = 10.120/100 chemistry procedures or 0.10 hours per chemistry procedure

Once a labor standard is established, the standard cost can be computed as follows:

$$\text{Standard unit labor cost} = \text{Standard time per unit of work} \times \text{Standard wage rate per hour}$$

and

$$\text{Standard total labor cost} = \text{Standard labor cost per unit of work} \times \text{Actual number of units of work for the period}$$

In this example, if the laboratory technologist's standard wage rate is $8.00 per hour, and he performs 250 chemistry procedures, the standard labor cost would be:

$$\text{Standard unit labor cost} = \$0.10 \times \$8.00 = \$0.80/\text{chemistry procedure}$$

and

$$\text{Standard total labor cost} = \$0.80 \times 250 = \$200.00$$

In addition to determining the standard labor cost of the 250 chemistry procedures, the labor standard can be used to determine standard labor utilization as follows:

$$\text{Standard total labor usage} = \text{Standard labor cost per unit of work} \times \text{Actual number of units of work for the period}$$

or

$$\text{Standard total labor usage} = 0.10 \times 250 = 25 \text{ standard hours}$$

In summary, the use of standards for all direct and transferred expenses can enhance the cost measurement process. An objective of the cost accounting system should be to measure costs in a manner that maximizes the classification of expenses into the direct expense and transferred expense classifications. Use of allocated expense or overhead category should be kept to a minimum. Responsibility accounting is enhanced by specific identification of responsibility. However, some allocation will always be necessary to fully cost hospital services. Therefore, the use of standards for allocated expenses is also a part of the standard cost system.

STANDARDS FOR TRANSFERRED OR ALLOCATED COSTS

In chapter 3, transferred and allocated costs are categorized as those costs accumulated in patient care support cost centers and in general and administrative cost centers. For the purpose of full absorption costing, transferred costs can be classified as variable expenses and allocated costs can be classified as fixed expenses. In this context, variable expenses are defined as those that can be matched with services rendered and therefore assigned to users of the services at a standard rate per service unit. The rate per service unit is not significantly affected by the level of capacity achieved by the hospital. Therefore, total transferred expenses fluctuate with volume of services performed.

Similarly, fixed allocated expenses are defined as those costs that, in total, do not significantly vary with the level of capacity achieved. However, because total costs do not vary, unit costs must, of necessity, change with the level of capacity achieved. If the level of capacity achieved is higher than that budgeted, the unit costs will be lower than those budgeted, and vice versa.

STANDARDS FOR THE TRANSFER OF VARIABLE COSTS

Chapter 3 refers to expenses that can be identified directly with services provided (transferred expenses) and expenses that cannot be identified as being directly applicable to patient services provided (allocated expenses). The following discussion explains the application of standards to the transfer and allocation of expenses. The laundry department is used as an example of a transferred expense (variable in relation to services provided) and the personnel department is used as an example of an allocated expense (fixed over a given range by hospital activity). Generally, variable expense standards are defined through a determination of the relationships between the use of the service and one or more outputs and resource inputs of the user cost center. This relationship usually takes the following form:

$$
\begin{array}{c}
\text{Total} \\
\text{utilization} \\
\text{volume} \\
\text{for a user} \\
\text{cost center}
\end{array}
=
\begin{array}{c}
\text{Constant number} \\
\text{of units used in} \\
\text{the cost center} \\
\text{each period} \\
\text{regardless of} \\
\text{activity level}
\end{array}
+
\left(
\begin{array}{c}
\text{Number of} \\
\text{units used per} \\
\text{unit of output} \\
\text{or input}
\end{array}
\times
\begin{array}{c}
\text{Actual} \\
\text{output or} \\
\text{input of} \\
\text{user cost} \\
\text{center}
\end{array}
\right)
$$

In order to further illustrate, assume the following:

U_{Vi} = Standard number of service units of a variable transferred expense utilized in cost center *(i)* (for example, pounds of laundry)

A_i = A constant number of service units per flexible performance reporting period for cost center *(i)* (for example, units per month), if any

B_i = Factors representing the use of a unit of variable service per unit of cost center *(i)* output or resource input (for example, 12.5 pounds of laundry per patient day)

X_i = User cost center *(i)* units of output(s) and resource input(s) (for example, patient days)

The formula can be expressed as follows:

$$U_{Vi} = A_i + B_i X_i$$

Because there may be more than one factor that represents the use of the service in a given department, additional factors can be added for each additional unit of variable service performed. The formula can then be expressed as follows:

$$U_{Vi} = A_i + B_i X_i + B^1{}_i X^1{}_i + B^2{}_i X^2{}_i$$

For example, for a nursing floor, a constant amount of laundry may be used just because the department is open for uniforms, gowns, and other garments. In addition, the amount of laundry will vary in accordance with the number of patient days and the number of discharges or transfers of patients from and to that unit. The above equation could then be expressed as follows:

Pounds of laundry = 1,500 pounds + 15 pounds/patient day × patient days + 30 pounds/discharge × number of discharges or transfers

Note that all factors in the equation may be user cost center specific. To a large extent, the factors in the equation are determined through the same management engineering techniques described earlier for the development of direct expense standards. In most instances, the variable transfer expense relationship will take the simple form:

$$U_{Vi} = B_i X_i$$

or

Pounds of laundry in user = Variable × Units
cost center   usage   of output
                             factor   and resource
                             for *i*   inputs for *i*

In this equation, a single relationship is used to measure the standard utilization of patient care support services. Although this approach may simplify the development of standards, it may make variance analysis (see chapter 10) more difficult if multiple utilization factors exist. Once the standard utilization of the variable services has been determined, the standard total cost *(C_V)* of those services can be defined as price or unit cost *(P_V)* times volume *(U_V)* or:

$$C_V = P_V \times U_V$$

Simply stated, total standard cost equals price per unit times the budgeted or estimated volume or number of units.

The standard price used to cost the variable service is the full absorption cost per service unit. It is the price that, after transfer and allocation of standard variable and fixed expense, provides for the standard cost of the service to be fully absorbed. Within the relevant range of budgeted capacity, this rate will remain constant except for minor fluctuations that result from spreading identified direct fixed costs over varying levels of service.

STANDARDS FOR THE ALLOCATION OF FIXED COSTS

Variable expense standards can be developed with some assurance because of identifiable service units. It is more difficult to establish standards for allocated expenses because fixed expenses cannot be identified with any specific service unit. Fixed service expense is generally the result of management providing a level of service related to some range of anticipated capacity.

For example, the total cost of a personnel department in a 300-bed hospital will be higher if the management anticipates an average census of 280 versus 140. However, the difference between the personnel department cost at 280 and the cost at 140 will probably not be twice as much. Because the use of personnel services by other departments does not relate directly to the census or other output measure, personnel service costs should be allocated on some basis that relates to the reason for the existence of the services (employees, in this case). This is an attempt to establish the basis for allocation on resource usage.

First, the appropriate resources to be used as the allocation base should be identified by hospital management. Then, overhead standards can be developed by management engineering or through other methods for resource usage per unit of output in departments receiving the allocation.

Using the personnel department as an example, management may determine that employees are the resource (expressed as labor hours) that best relates to the allocation of personnel service costs. If a cost center uses labor hours, it should incur a portion of these personnel service costs. The standard usage of personnel services could then be stated in terms of standard labor hours earned. In other words, any hospital department that uses labor to deliver patient services or provide support services has earned an appropriate share of the personnel department's cost (at a standard rate per hour of labor used). The number of hours used to compute the total transfer to the individual departments is referred to as the standard labor hours earned. This can be expressed as:

The standard number of resource units for fixed overhead	$=$	The standard resource usage per unit of the user cost center output	$\times$	The actual user cost center

The above equation can be expressed as:

$$U_{Fi} = R_i \times V_i$$

where:

U_{Fi} = Standard number of resource units for a fixed overhead service (for example, standard total labor hours).

R_i = Standard resource usage per unit of user cost center *(i)* output (for example, standard labor hours per patient day).

V_i = Actual user cost center *(i)* output (for example, patient days).

The standard fixed overhead service cost *(C_F)* incurred is similarly determined through the use of a unit price or overhead "burden" rate *(P_F)* times actual volume *(U_F)* of resources used, or:

$$C_F = P_F \times U_F$$

The establishment of the standard "burden" rate (sometimes called the fixed overhead application rate) is complicated by the fact that the amount of fixed costs allocated will vary as the level of achieved capacity changes. The costing question raised is how is an appropriate single burden rate for applying fixed overhead determined? The answer is found in reviewing management's rationale for setting the level of resources consumed for these services. In most instances, the cost of these services is predicated on the achievement of a specified level of capacity for the hospital. This level of capacity is used to produce the standard budget (standard cost at the predetermined level of capacity). Therefore, the standard burden rate for each fixed overhead service can be defined as follows:

$$P_F = \frac{C_F}{U_F}$$

or

Standard fixed overhead burden rate	=	Standard cost of the fixed overhead service @ standard budget capacity	÷	Standard budget number of allocation base resource units for the fixed overhead service

Using the personnel department services as an example, the standard burden rate should be $0.08 per labor hour if management has determined that, for budget purposes, a specified occupancy of 90 percent will be achieved and that, at this level, the standard cost of providing personnel services should be $120,000. In addition, at the 90-percent level all hospital services would require labor resources of 1,500,000 standard labor hours. In this case, the standard burden rate was computed as follows:

Personnel service burden rate	=	$\dfrac{\$120,000}{1,500,000 \text{ labor hours}}$	=	$0.08/labor hour

If a nursing unit has an occupancy rate of 8,000 patient days and is using 5.00 standard labor hours per patient day, the standard personnel department service overhead of $3,200 would be computed as follows:

Standard labor hours per patient day	$\times$	8,000 patient days	$=$	The standard volume of labor resources used

or

$$5.00 \times 8,000 = 40,000 \text{ standard labor hours}$$

and

Standard personnel rate per standard labor hour	$\times$	Standard labor hours	$=$	Standard personnel services overhead cost for the nursing unit

or

$$\$0.08 \times 40,000 = \$3,200$$

In summary, standards must be determined for both transferred and overhead expenses. For transferred expenses, the standard should be based on the relationship between use of a particular service and the inputs and outputs of the user. In the case of allocated expenses (overhead), standards should be based on resource inputs most directly related to the purpose for using a particular service. In both instances, the standards should be costed at a standard price. For transferred expense, the price should be the full absorption cost per service unit. However, for allocated expense, the price should be based on the standard cost at the standard budget level of resource utilization.

PURPOSE OF TRANSFER AND ALLOCATED COSTING

There are two basic, correlated reasons why a hospital should concern itself with transfer and allocated cost standards. First, transfer and allocated costing provides a means for each member of the management team to participate in the control of the cost of services necessary for the functioning of the hospital but not directly involved in the provision of patient care. Second, it prescribes the nature of the responsibility for these costs to the providing and using cost centers.

Through these standards, user department managers have an opportunity to investigate the key factors in the incurrence of these costs, to investigate the relationships of these costs to the quality of patient care, and, above all, to investigate alternative methods and procedures that could potentially reduce overhead costs incurred or increase the quality of service in their area. These activities, made possible by the process of setting and maintaining transfer and allocated cost standards, provide management with an aspect of control previously unavailable through traditional accounting and cost finding.

Procedure for Charging Transfer and Allocated Costs

The purpose of transfer and allocated costing is to provide a means for all management to participate in the control of overhead costs. The development of provider and user department standards is the first step in achieving that purpose. The second step is the analysis of variances between standard overhead costs and actual or actual allocated costs. As the analysis of variance is the subject of chapter 10, this chapter will concern itself with the procedures for charging transfers and allocated service expense. As stated in chapter 6, the purpose of transferring and allocating expense is to achieve full costing of patient services. With the use of a standard cost accounting system, the purpose of charging these expenses is to achieve greater management control, although a means for providing for the full costing of patient services must also be made available. Because the transfers and allocations are made at a standard price, the amounts transferred and allocated may be less than, equal to, or greater than the actual total cost.

The amount of service expense transferred (C_V) will equal the standard price per service unit (P_V) times the actual units of service consumed (U_V) plus the error term or the amount over- or under-applied (E). This can be expressed as:

$$C_{V\ (actual)} = P_V \times U_{V\ (actual)} + E$$

To illustrate this concept, the laundry service can be used as a representative service to be transferred to the user departments, as illustrated in table 10, below.

Table 10. Laundry Service Summary Management Control Report

	Actual costs	Standard costs	*Flexible performace variance
Volume = 61,200 lb.			
Direct expenses	$12,000	$10,000	$2,000U*
Transferred expenses	3,000	3,500	500F*
Allocated expenses	2,000	1,800	200U
	17,000	$15,300	$1,700U
Amount transferred @ $0.25/pound	15,300		
Under (over) applied	$ 1,700		

*Flexible performance reports are discussed in chapter 11.   F = favorable; U = unfavorable.

From this simplified illustration, it should be apparent that generally the amount of expense transferred to user departments is equal to the standard cost of the service at the actual volume of service rendered. As a result, the flexible performance variance is the key control item for the laundry department manager in obtaining full absorption of his costs by the user departments.

The amount of overhead expense allocated $(C_{F\ [actual]})$ is equal to the standard price or burden rate (P_F) times the actual number of units of the resource used $(U_{F\ [actual]})$. If there is variance, E can be used to signify the amount over or under applied. This can be expressed as follows:

$$C_{F\ (actual)} = P_F \times U_{F\ (actual)} + E$$

Using the personnel department, the allocation of overhead costs is illustrated in table 11 and table 12, below.

Table 11. Personnel Service Summary Management Control Report, Example 1

	Actual costs	Standard costs	Flexible performance variance
Volume = 1,500,000 labor hours			
Direct expenses	$83,000	$80,000	$3,000 U
Transferred expenses	19,000	20,000	1,000 F
Allocated expenses	23,000	20,000	3,000 U
	$125,000	$120,000	$5,000 U
Amount allocated @ $0.08/labor hour	120,000		
Under (over) applied	$5,000		

In table 11, which is very similar to the transfer expense illustration, actual usage of the resource used as the allocation base (labor hours) is equal to the standard budget amount on which the standard burden rate was established (1,500,000 labor hours). Hence, the total overhead allocated was equal to the standard cost of the service. However, in most instances, actual base resource usage is not equal to that used to establish the standard burden rate, as shown in table 12, below.

Table 12. Personnel Service Summary Management Control Report, Example 2

	Actual costs	Standard costs	Flexible performance variance
Volume = 1,350,000 labor hours			
Total expense	$125,000	$120,000	$5,000 U
Amount allocated @ $0.08/labor hour	108,000		
Under (over) applied	$17,000		

Table 12 uncovers the major weaknesses in using unit rates for fixed overhead costs. Actual usage of the resource base in this example was only 1,350,000 labor hours instead of 1,500,000 labor hours as used in the standard budget to determine the burden rate. Because of this, a variance in the amount of overhead allocated to other departments of $12,000 occurs computed as follows:

$$Q_F = \left(\begin{array}{l} \text{Actual usage of} \\ \text{the resource} \end{array} - \begin{array}{l} \text{Standard usage of} \\ \text{the resource base} \end{array} \right) \times \begin{array}{l} \text{Standard burden} \\ \text{rate} \end{array}$$

$$Q_F = \left(\begin{array}{l} 1,350,000 \text{ labor} \\ \text{hours} \end{array} - \begin{array}{l} 1,500,000 \text{ labor} \\ \text{hours} \end{array} \right) \times \begin{array}{l} \$0.80/\text{per labor} \\ \text{hour} \end{array}$$

$$= \underline{\underline{\$12,000\text{U}}}$$

Total variance = $ 5,000 Flexible performance variance (U)
$\phantom{\text{Total variance} =}$ <u>12,000</u> Allocated overhead variance (U)
$\phantom{\text{Total variance} =}$ <u>$17,000U</u>

Note that, in the true sense, the $5,000 flexible variance can be caused by price or efficiency, and the $12,000 burden rate variance is caused by volume. This will be discussed in greater detail in chapter 11.

Although personnel department costs are determined in relation to a planned level of service, the amount of personnel service burden allocated varies with the difference between actual and standard use of the resource designated as the base for determining the unit cost of the service. Furthermore, there is little, if anything, the providing department manager can do to change the actual usage of the base resource. Use of this resource is related to the hospital achievement of its capacity goals and to each department manager's ability to efficiently use the resources under his control with respect to standard use for actual output achieved.

As discussed at the beginning of this section, the purpose for transferring and allocating expenses at standard rates is to improve management control through flexible performance reporting and variance analysis. However, all costs must be fully absorbed by the patient care services if appropriate service pricing decisions are to be made. Therefore, the standard cost accounting system must also provide a means for allocating the variances to revenue-producing cost centers. There are many ways in which this can be accomplished, several of the more pertinent techniques are as follows:

- Reapply transferred and overhead expenses based on actual cost per service unit or actual burden rate.
- Allocate variances to revenue-producing cost centers only in proportion to expenses absorbed at the standard prices.
- Allocate variances to revenue-producing cost centers based on other criteria such as gross revenue, cost, and so forth.
- Allocate variances evenly to revenue-producing cost centers.

The advantages and disadvantages of each of these methods is beyond the scope of this text. Suffice it to say that hospital management will have to choose and provide for an appropriate method under the individual hospital's circumstances of obtaining the full cost of revenue-producing services. If standards are set realistically and maintained properly, the variance amount should be minor compared with the hospital's total cost, thus minimizing any problems associated with the allocation of the variances.

CHAPTER **9**

Flexible Performance Reports

In order to receive maximum benefit from cost accounting, cost data must be communicated to management accurately, at timely intervals, and in a useful format. Performance reports, which provide information for review and decision making, should direct management's attention to situations that are out of control. Performance reports are control mechanisms that stimulate management to take corrective action.

Once a proper standard cost has been determined, managers can dismiss the question of cost from their mind until there is a variance between actual cost and standard cost. When a significant variation in cost occurs, managers should be able to analyze and determine where it occurred, who was responsible, and why it happened. Appropriate steps can be taken to eliminate the cause of the variance through operational improvements, strengthened control, or whatever.

A flexible performance reporting system provides appropriate levels of management with data that can be used to:
- Measure and control labor performance
- Determine the effectiveness of supervisory control over work performed, supplies used, and so forth
- Identify areas needing corrective action or improvement
- Identify areas in which special management studies might be needed to develop alternative courses of action or to implement decisions
- Highlight spending level and supply usage changes related to amounts of services rendered
- Analyze the effect of volume changes on the ability of the hospital to absorb fixed costs
- Measure or predict the impact of changes in case mix, payer mix or activity levels.

LEVELS OF REPORTING

A separate cost center should be established at the lowest organizational element that has a supervised function or activity. Line-item accounts within specified classifications should be maintained for each cost center. The accounts should be charged with all costs that can be directly related to the functions or activities of that organizational element.

As discussed in section II, cost centers should be grouped and combined according to the management hierarchy delineated for the organization. A system of performance reporting should be established on the same basis. Performance reports can then be prepared for individual cost centers and should thus reflect only the costs and volumes directly related to the function or activity in that cost center. Performance reporting on this basis facilitates the management principle of clear delineation and delegation of responsibility. The person charged with the responsibilty for the management of supervision of persons performing a specified function or activity can be held accountable for achieving a desired level of performance.

Figure 22, next page, illustrates the relationships between the organizational structure and the reporting system. The system operates as follows:

- Results of operations are reported through the hospital's organizational structure by a multilevel management and financial reporting system: activity reports, function reports, cost center reports, departmental reports, administrative reports, and hospitalwide reports.
- Responsible managers from each organizational level analyze and explain variance each month and report findings to their superior.
- Corrective actions are taken in situations requiring management control. These actions may result from decisions reached by department managers, by conferences with supervisors and their superiors, or from recommendations resulting from special management studies.

The performance reporting system is responsibility reporting. It should provide each manager with only the performance evaluation data pertinent to his defined responsibility, as delineated in the plan or organization.

At any functional level, the reports should compare the actual cost of the function with the expected level of cost on the basis of actual volume of activity for that function. Actual material, labor, and indirect costs are accumulated and compared with an earned budget. This budget is calculated by multiplying the volume of activity by standards established for material, labor, and indirect costs for the major activities comprising the function.

Each level above the functional level receives a report summarizing the results of those units reporting to it. For example, at the division level (clinical pathology) in the example in figure 22, the three units reporting to the division manager—chemistry, hematology, and microbiology—are shown on a divisional report, which reflects actual financial results, earned budget, and variance for the activity in those units. These results are moved up the organization structure level by level to produce an overall hospital financial report. A similar set of staffing reports employing the same responsibility reporting concept are also produced. The major advantages of this reporting approach are:

- Individuals in the organization are made responsible and held accountable for cost or revenue performance.
- Standards are developed that provide meaningful measures of performance.
- Performance is reported to specific individuals who exercise control over costs or revenues.
- Individuals are held responsible for those activities over which they exercise direct control.

FLEXIBLE REPORTING

The technique for performance reporting using standard costs is called flexible performance reporting (flexible budgeting). To understand how flexible reporting works, it is necessary to understand cost behavior patterns, which are discussed in detail in chapter 2. A brief review of the chapter is appropriate.

Costs have behavior patterns that relate to volume of activity. Variable costs are those that increase in total as volume increases. Fixed costs are those that remain the same in total regardless of volume. Figure 23, page 86, presents this relationship in a simple graph.

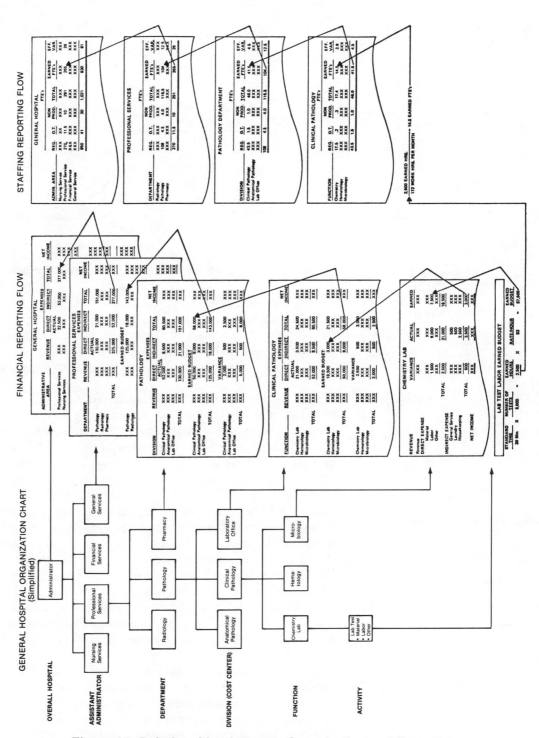

Figure 22. Relationships between Organization and Reporting

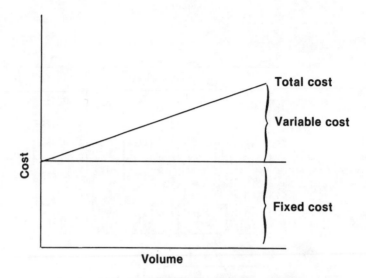

Figure 23. Fixed Costs versus Variable Costs

Total cost at a given level of volume is the fixed cost plus the variable cost for that volume of activity. As described in chapter 2, because all costs do not fall into the pure fixed or pure variable category, there are some problems in classifying cost in this manner. However, if standards are determined through careful analysis, a reasonable relationship between variable costs and volume can be established.

The variable performance goal is set by using the standard cost for a service unit and relating that to the actual volume of activity for each reporting period. Therefore, the goal or standard cost (standard budget) for a given cost center for a given period will increase or decrease in relation to the actual level of activity. The standard performance goal is an attempt to duplicate the total cost line with expectations for total cost for a predetermined level of efficiency.

. The flexible standard budget is determined retroactively. The standard performance, in terms of total expenditure allowed, is determined at the end of the period and is based on what should have been expended (inputs) to produce the actual services rendered (outputs). Consider the example in figure 24, next page.

If a fixed budget were used to measure the cost behavior and the volume level were established at the beginning of the period to be X_2 (500 patient days), the budget would be set at Y_2 ($42,500), regardless of the volume of services actually provided. This would limit the usefulness of the reports to situations in which the volume did not fluctuate from the budgeted volume (X_2). At an actual volume of X_1 (400 patient days) and a fixed budget Y_2 ($42,500), a favorable situation may be perceived that is inaccurate. Conversely, at an actual volume of X_3 (600 patient days) and a fixed budget at Y_2 ($42,500), an unfavorable variance may be perceived in error.

The flexible standard goal (standard budget) is intended to set performance standards at the appropriate level of expenditure for the actual volume of activity that occurred, thus eliminating the effect of volume. This enables management to more accurately measure the other factors that cause variances, such as price, labor rate, or inefficient use of labor and supplies.

Nursing Floor

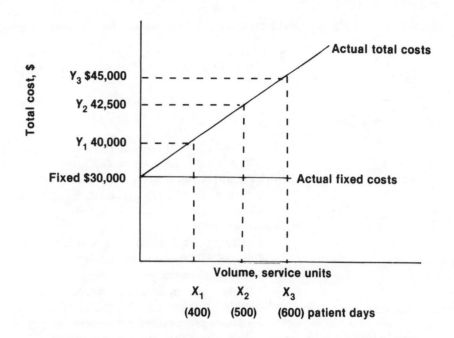

Figure 24. Fixed Budget versus Flexible Standard Budget

To illustrate the preparation of a flexible performance report, consider the following example for a pediatrics nursing floor.

Pediatrics Floor, Month, Year
Actual results for the month
    20 beds available
    16 = average daily census
    480 actual patient days
    96 patient discharges
Standards
Direct expense
    Supervisor = 1.4 Full-time equivalent (FTE) employees (7-day coverage) = $2,500/month (fixed)
    RNs = 1.3 hours per patient day at $6.50 per hour
    LPNs = 1.7 hours per patient day at $5.00 per hour
    Nursing assistants = 0.9 hours per patient day at $3.25 per hour
    Supplies-inventory = 10 items per patient day at $0.20 per item
    Supplies-noninventory = $300 per month (fixed)
    Pediatrician's fees = 0.5 hours per patient day at $10.00 per hour
    Other direct expense = $250 per month (fixed)
Transferred expense (support services)
    Laundry = (1,500 pounds + 15 pounds per patient day + 30 pounds per discharge) at $0.25 per pound

Allocated expense (general indirect services)
Personnel department = 242 hours (fixed for supervisor) + 3.9 hours per patient day (for RNs, LPNs, and so forth) at $0.08 per hour

Given the actual results and standards for the pediatrics floor, the flexible performance goals (standards) for the month would be computed as follows:

Supervisor
The standard is fixed at $2,500 per month
RNs
1.3 hours × 480 patient days = 624 standard hours
624 × $6.50 per hour = $4,056
LPNs
1.7 hours × 480 patient days = 816 standard hours
816 × $5.00 per hour = $4,080
Nursing assistants
0.9 hours × 480 patient days = 432 standard hours
432 × $3.25 per hour = $1,404
Supplies-inventory
10 items × 480 patient days = 4,800 standard items
4,800 × $0.20 per item = $960
Supplies-noninventory
The standard is fixed at $300 per month
Pediatrician's fees
0.5 hours per patient day × 480 = 240 standard hours
240 × $10.00 per hour = $2,400
Other direct expense
The standard is fixed at $240 per month
Laundry
This standard has three components:
1. Constant amount is 1,500 pounds at $0.25   = $ 375
2. 15 pounds × 480 patient days = 7,200 pounds
   7,200 × $102.5 per pound   = 1,800
3. 30 pounds × 96 discharges = 2,800 pounds
   2,800 × $0.25 per pound   = 720
   Total standard laundry expense   = $2,895

Personnel services

This standard has two components:
1. Constant amount is 242 hours at $0.08 per hour   = $ 19.36
2. 3.9 hours × 480 patient days = 1,872 standard hours
   1,872 × $0.08 per hour   = 149.76
   Total standard for personnel services   = $169.12

Table 13, next page, illustrates a monthly performance report for the pediatrics nursing floor using the standards computed in the last example. There are support services in the performance report for which no computation is illustrated. These would be computed on some basis comparable to the computations that are shown. The actual figures represent the actual expense recorded for the period and the total variances are disclosed. The analysis of variances is discussed in chapter 10.

Table 13. Monthly Performance Report for a Pediatrics Nursing Floor

	Actual	Standard	Variance
Service units			
Patient days	480		
Average daily census	16		
Patient discharges	96		
Direct expenses			
Salaries and wages:			
Supervisors	$ 2,500	$ 2,500	0
RNs	4,320	4,056	$ 264U[a]
LPNs	3,763	4,080	317F[a]
Nursing assts.	1,680	1,404	276U
Supplies—inventory	825	960	135F
Supplies—noninventory	520	300	220U
Pediatrician fees	3,158	2,400	758U
Other direct expenses	275	250	25U
Total direct expense	17,041	15,950	1,091U
Support service expenses (applied)			
Housekeeping	880	960	80F
Laundry	3,000	2,895	105U
Maintenance	1,800	1,440	360U
Total support expenses	5,680	5,295	385U
Indirect Expenses (applied)			
Personnel	176	169	7U
Other administrative and general	898	858	40U
Total indirect expenses	1,074	1,027	47U
Total department expense	$23,795	$22,272	$1,523U

[a] F = favorable variance; U = unfavorable variance.

DECISION MAKING

Control and decision making over costs is most effectively exercised through action at the source. Quantity of materials utilized should be controlled by the user. Labor performance is best controlled at the cost center in which personnel are assigned. On the other hand, quality and price of materials should be controlled at the time of purchase.

Variances in labor costs can be attributed to differences between actual and standard labor rates and differences between the standard and actual time to complete an activity. Variances in material prices can be caused by purchasing in nonstandard lots or from unfavorably located suppliers, thereby increasing transportation expenditures. Other causes might be market price fluctuation, failure to take advantage of discounts, theft, loss in material usage as a result of waste, or changes in product specifications not incorporated into the standard. Variances in overhead costs can be attributed to spending more or less than budgeted for the actual hours operated. They also are caused by changes in the volumes of allocation bases from budget. For example, if personnel is allocated on the basis of labor hours at a standard budget rate and hours are above or below the standard budget, there will be an overhead volume variance.

The performance reporting system should routinely measure the work output of various departments, groups of employees, or individuals. The reporting of this information is critical in spotlighting problem areas and facilitating the correction of these problems. If performance falls below the anticipated goal, management should initiate a systematic program of investigation and analysis, followed by any necessary corrective action. This program might consist of the following:

- Compare methods followed in performing procedures against methods described in time standard methodology
- Compare work place layout with suggested layout in time standard development
- Compare average batch size to standard batch size, if appropriate
- Check reporting of volume counts and actual hours worked
- Analyze staffing and scheduling patterns
- Analyze fluctuations in case mix and the responsible manager's effectiveness in responding to them

If all the aforementioned checks indicate the department or its employees should have attained the performance goal but failed to do so, the supervisor should discuss the situation with those personnel being measured and provide them with the motivation for improving work patterns and output.

Flexible performance reports provide a tool with which to measure actual performance against specified objectives and to highlight those areas in which there are either problems with the standards or causes of departure from standard. However, variances, as stated here, may occur as the result of a multiplicity of factors, for example:

- Length of stay
- Price of input factors
- Case mix
- Efficiencies
- Seasonal factors

The cost accounting system provides the ability to gather and display the information required to analyze and predict cost behavior patterns as they fluctuate with volume. The system does so by the use of standards, which can be looked at as the "budget" for a specific unit of output within a relevant range. We can now examine these causes for departure from our flexible performance objectives, which are necessarily separate and distinct from changes in the volume of services provided.

It may be wise to review the examples of nonvolume-related variances that are discussed in the beginning of chapter 2. The advantage in a cost accounting system is that managers can address discrepancies in actual behavior from planned behavior with tools that not only measure the magnitude of a discrepancy but also highlight the causes.

The next chapter presents the final component to complete a cost accounting system: variance analysis. Variance analysis provides managers with a means of focusing on a specific cause of variance so that they might investigate the cause and exert management control where possible. Variance analysis is the key to achieving maximum effectiveness in the utilization of managerial cost accounting.

CHAPTER 10

Variance Analysis

Variance is simply defined as any difference between the flexible performance objective and the actual performance attained in any measurable unit. It is equal to the difference between standard cost and actual cost in a specific department, unit, function, or line item. A variance is considered unfavorable when actual costs are greater than standard costs. Similarly, a variance is considered favorable when actual costs are less than standard costs. Variances can be calculated for cost centers, functions, natural expense classifications, or specific departmental line items. The greater the degree of precision or detail employed in calculating variances, the more information is provided to managers as to the cause of variances.

The multiplicity of factors that cause fluctuations in cost behavior can deter the manager from attempting to identify and explain them. Cost accounting texts may list as many as 15 or 20 distinct causes of variance and provide detailed equations for their calculation. For the purpose of instruction, we will present seven primary types of variances, which reflect the major reasons for fluctuations from standard. Once these types are understood, the manager can further refine his determination of the causes of variance, as he sees fit.

The seven variances are:

Direct costs
1. Price/rate variances
   a. Labor rate variance
   b. Nonlabor price variance
2. Usage/efficiency variances
   a. Labor efficiency variance
   b. Nonlabor usage variance

Transferred costs
3. Price/rate variance (Transfer rate variance)
4. Usage/efficiency variance (Usage variance)

Allocated costs
5. Price/rate variance (Allocated rate variance)
6. Usage/efficiency variance (Usage variance)
7. Overhead application (Volume variance)

Variance analysis is the determination of the causes or sources of variance. It is applied to variances of direct, transferred, or indirect costs. The performing of variance analysis can be problematic, as the causes of variance can be difficult to distinguish from one another. In the example of seasonal variance in chapter 2, the manager observes that there are seasonal changes in the cost of fresh produce. These changes have caused a price variance in the line item of produce in the dietary department and a rate variance in transferred meal costs in the patient care areas.

To perform variance analysis, it is first necessary to understand the standards. A manager must be reasonably satisfied that the standards accurately measure current utilization of labor, supplies, support, and overhead services. The standards should be priced to reflect current conditions, both internal (wage scales) and external (inflation) to the hospital; actual costs should be appropriately identified through the hospital's cost accounting systems. It is also necessary to determine responsibility for variances and ensure that managers are exercising effort to control their sources or causes.

Management should also assess their ability to control the variables or conditions that are causing the variance. To the extent that variances can be controlled by a department manager, he should prepare a plan that describes how such control can be achieved. If the causes or sources of variances are uncontrollable or controllable by others, plans should be initiated that will provide the department manager with more control through appropriate changes in hospital policies, procedures, and operations.

There are two objectives of this chapter: first, to present the primary types of variances arising from the use of standard costs in flexible budgeting and reporting; and second, to describe the process of variance analysis and depict its key role in a system of management control. A further and more detailed discussion of the effective use of a cost accounting system is presented in chapter 11.

As stated in chapter 9, a cost accounting system allows managers to analyze each of the causes of variances in isolation. Supervisors and managers of all levels now have the information required to exercise management control over expenditures and to account for variances in their areas. They will also have measurable objectives to assist them in fulfilling their portion of the hospital's operational plan.

PRICE/RATE AND USAGE/EFFICIENCY VARIANCES

As previously described, variance is defined as the difference between actual cost and standard cost. In overall terms, the total standard cost would be the standard budget computed from standard resource usage or inputs (hours of labor, units or supplies, and so forth) at standard prices (rates) for the budgeted output of the hospital. The problem with this definition is that the resulting variance combines too many elements (volume of output, price, and resource usage) to render it useful for the purpose of management control. It can expressed as:

$$\text{Variance} = \text{Standard cost} - \text{Actual cost}$$

or

$$\text{Variance} = (\text{Standard price} \times \text{Standard quantity})$$
$$- \text{Actual price} \times \text{Actual quantity})$$

It is readily apparent that there are only two components that will fluctuate: price and quantity. They can be stated algebraically:

Price/Rate variance = Actual quantity × (Standard price − actual price)
Usage/Efficiency variance = Standard price × (Standard quantity used − Actual quantity used)

The sum of these variances is equivalent to the original equation, or:

Price/Rate variance + Usage/Efficiency variance = Total variance

These equations will be used repeatedly throughout this chapter. There is only one variance presented that cannot be calculated from these equations, the volume variance that occurs when predicted volume of output is different from actual volume used for the application of fixed overhead. This will be addressed in the section on allocated costs.

FLEXIBLE PERFORMANCE REPORTS AND BUDGET VARIANCES

The following example depicts the need for flexible performance reports in refining the concept of variance. A hospital's budget called for 100,000 patient days. On the basis of departmental standards established for resource utilization and the price or rate per unit of resource, the hospital determined a standard cost of $200 per patient day, or a total standard budget cost of $20,000,000. When this is compared with the actual cost of $18,975,000 at 90,000 actual patient days, the $1,025,000 variance cannot be readily explained. What should have been spent at a level of output of 90,000 patient days? Was more or less paid than should have been paid for the resources used at the 90,000 patient-day level?

The answers are obtained through the use of flexible performance reports and the development of appropriate subvariances in order to measure resource usage (efficiency) and price (rate) deviations from the standard. Flexible performance reports enable the hospital to recompute the standard budget on the basis of actual output. Using the standards developed, the hospital now determines a standard cost of $205 per patient day at the level of 90,000 patient days. The $5.00 increase in the cost per patient day results from the fixed costs being spread over a level of output less than the budgeted amount. To illustrate:

Actual costs (90,000 patient days)	**Flexible performance report** (90,000 patient days)	**Standard budget** (100,000 patient days)
$18,975,000	$18,450,000	$20,000,000

Flexible budget variance	**Standard budget variance**
$525,000 unfavorable	$1,550,000 favorable

The flexible performance report provides an answer to the question concerning what should have been spent at the actual level of output produced. In addition, if combined with an analysis of associated revenues, the real volume effect on income of attaining an output different from the standard budget can be determined. For instance, in the preceding example, if the standard revenue per patient day was $205, net income would have been $205 × 100,000 = $20,500,000 − $20,000,000 = $500,000 at standard. If actual patient days were 90,000, the flexible budget net income would have been $205 × 90,000 = $18,450,000 − $18,450,000 = $0. In summary, the use of the flexible performance report also provides hospital managers with a means of assessing the impact of changes in output on the net income of the hospital.

The flexible performance report isolates the volume variance between the standard budget and the flexible performance report at actual output. It also provides the base for measuring price and usage variances, which together form the flexible performance report variance. The analysis of these variances is the basic technique for exercising management control with a cost accounting system using standard costs.

VARIANCES IN DIRECT COSTS

In a department's direct costs, there are two types of variances, price/rate and usage/efficiency, which can be applied to labor and nonlabor costs. Thus, with respect to direct labor costs, not only is the manpower used (stated in hours) important, but so is the cost of each one of those hours in relation to the standard. In order to explain a labor cost variance, it may be necessary to analyze wage rates, premium pay, shift differentials, and other wage factors, in addition to the quantity or type of personnel used. In nonlabor direct expenses, the quantity used and the unit price are major factors in determining the causes or sources of variances. In this area, such factors as waste, inflation, and changes in products used should also be considered in explaining the variances.

Consistent with the formulas shown earlier, these variances are defined as follows:

Labor rate variance (P_L)

$$P_L = \begin{array}{c} \text{Actual hours} \\ \text{worked} \end{array} \times \left(\begin{array}{c} \text{Standard wage} \\ \text{rate per hour} \end{array} - \begin{array}{c} \text{Actual wage} \\ \text{rate per hour} \end{array} \right)$$

Labor efficiency variance (Q_L)

$$Q_L = \begin{array}{c} \text{Standard wage} \\ \text{rate per hour} \end{array} \times \left[\left(\begin{array}{c} \text{Actual units} \\ \text{of output} \end{array} \times \begin{array}{c} \text{Standard hours per} \\ \text{unit of output} \end{array} \right) - \begin{array}{c} \text{Actual hours} \\ \text{worked} \end{array} \right]$$

Nonlabor expense price variance (P_N)

$$P_N = \begin{array}{c} \text{Actual units of} \\ \text{particular} \\ \text{input purchased} \end{array} \times \left(\begin{array}{c} \text{Standard price} \\ \text{per unit of} \\ \text{particular} \\ \text{expense} \end{array} - \begin{array}{c} \text{Actual price per} \\ \text{unit of particular} \\ \text{input} \end{array} \right)$$

Nonlabor expense usage variance (Q_N)

$$Q_N = \begin{array}{c} \text{Standard price} \\ \text{per unit of} \\ \text{particular input} \end{array} \times \left[\left(\begin{array}{c} \text{Actual} \\ \text{units of} \\ \text{output} \end{array} \times \begin{array}{c} \text{Standard units of} \\ \text{particular input} \\ \text{per unit of output} \end{array} \right) - \begin{array}{c} \text{Actual units} \\ \text{of particular} \\ \text{input used} \end{array} \right]$$

Note that each price/rate variance is calculated as the difference in actual price or wage rate from standard times the actual wage usage of the input factor. Similarly, each usage/efficiency variance is the difference between actual usage of labor or supplies and the standard usage (at the actual level of volume achieved) times the standard price established for each.

In a hospital, the calculation of these variances for each line item may be difficult and occasionally impossible. However, labor rate and efficiency variances can usually be derived from the data provided through most payroll or personnel accounting systems. Similarly, most inventory control or accounts payable systems provide sufficient price and usage data to compute nonlabor variances, at least for those items maintained in inventory. The price and usage variances for medical fees of hospital-based physicians can be analyzed from data available through the hospital patient accounting system. For other types of expenses, if unit prices or quantities do not exist or cannot be recorded cost-effectively, variances may have to be analyzed in total, without the benefit of a price and usage comparison. However, in most hospitals, these expenses encompass only 10 to 20 percent of the total expenses of the hospital.

To illustrate the computation of variances, table 14, below, is the example used in chapter 9. The analysis of direct expenses is shown first. Transferred and overhead expenses are discussed later in this chapter.

Table 14. Pediatrics Floor Monthly Performance Report, Including Variances

	Actual	Standard	Variance	Price/ rate	Usage/ efficiency
Service units:					
Patient days	480				
Average daily census	16				
Patient discharges	96				
Direct expenses					
Salaries and wages:					
Supervisors	$ 2,500	$ 2,500	0	0	0
RNs	4,320	4,056	$ 264U[a]	$360F[a]	$624U
LPNs	3,763	4,080	317F	77F	240F
Nursing assts.	1,680	1,404	276U	120U	156U
Supplies — inventory	825	960	135F	135F	0
Supplies — non-inventory	520	300	220U	—	—
Pediatrician fees	3,158	2,400	758U	278U	480U
Other direct expenses	275	250	25U	—	—
Total direct expense	$17,041	$15,950	$1,091U		

[a] F = favorable; U = unfavorable

The variances shown in table 14 represent the difference between actual expenses incurred and the flexible performance goals (budgets) at the actual level of output. In this situation, actual output of the pediatrics unit was 480 patient days. The price/rate and usage/efficiency variances were computed according to the definitions given earlier in this section. For example, the RN salary variance is computed from the following information:

RN standard hours per unit of output = 1.3 hours per patient day
RN standard wage rate per hour = $6.50 per hour
RN actual hours used = 720 hours
RN actual wage rate per hour = $6.00 per hour ($4,320 + 720 hours)
RN labor rate variance (P_L) = 720 hours × ($6.50 per hour − $6.00 per hour)
    = $360 (favorable variance)
RN labor efficiency variance (Q_L) = $6.50 per hour ×

$$\left[\left(480 \text{ patient days} \times 1.3 \, \frac{\text{Standard hours}}{\text{Patient day}} \right) - 720 \text{ hours} \right]$$

= $624 (unfavorable variance)

The other direct labor variances for LPNs and nursing assistants are computed in this manner.

The inventory supplies variances are computed as follows:

Standard units of supplies per unit of output = 10 units per patient day
Standard price per unit of supply = $0.20 per unit
Actual units of supplies used = 4,800 units
Actual price per unit of supply = $0.172 per unit ($825 ÷ 4,800 units)
Inventory supplies price variance (P_N) = 4,800 units × ($0.20 per unit − $0.172 per unit) = $135 (favorable variance)
Inventory supplies usage variance (Q_N) = $0.20 per unit ×

$$\left[\left(480 \text{ patient days} \times 10 \ \frac{\text{Standard units}}{\text{Patient day}}\right) - 4,800 \text{ units}\right] = 0 \text{ (no variance)}$$

The variances for the pediatrician fees can be computed in a similar manner:

Standard service units per unit of output = 0.5 hours per patient day
Standard price per service unit = $10.00 per hour
Actual service units used = 288 hours
Actual price per service unit = $10.956 per hour ($3,158 ÷ 288 hours)
Pediatrician rate variance (P_N) = ($10.00 per hour − $10.965 per hour) × 288 hours = $278 (unfavorable)
Pediatrician efficiency variance (Q_N) =

$$\left[\left(480 \text{ patient days} \times 0.5 \ \frac{\text{Standard hours}}{\text{Patient day}}\right) - 288 \text{ hours}\right] \times \$10.00 \text{ per hour}$$

$$= \$480 \text{ (unfavorable)}$$

These computations of variances for labor and nonlabor expenses can be presented pictorially. Figure 25, next page, illustrates the relationship of the variances to the flexible performance report.

The variance analysis prepared by the pediatric unit supervisor for the director of nursing might read as follows:

- **Direct labor.** During the previous month, my unit picked up three newly recruited RNs, replacing two RNs who had retired. The new RNs were at the entry level on the pay scale, and the average hourly salary for all RNs on the unit was reduced to $6.00 per hour, resulting in a favorable labor rate variance. However, the replacing of two RNs with three RNs increased my RN nursing hours per patient day to 1.5 hours, resulting in an unfavorable labor efficiency variance at last month's average daily census. To compensate for the increased RN staffing, one LPN was transferred to 8 west. This resulted in both a favorable rate and efficiency variance for LPNs. However, in six months, when the new RNs reach the next pay level, the favorable rate variance will be lost resulting in a new RN plus LPN variance that is unfavorable. Therefore, I recommend that plans be made to replace one RN with one LPN.

  For a period of five consecutive days in the middle of the month, the unit ran a census of 20 patients. This required the use of 48 overtime hours for the nurse attendants, causing an unfavorable rate and efficiency variance for this group.

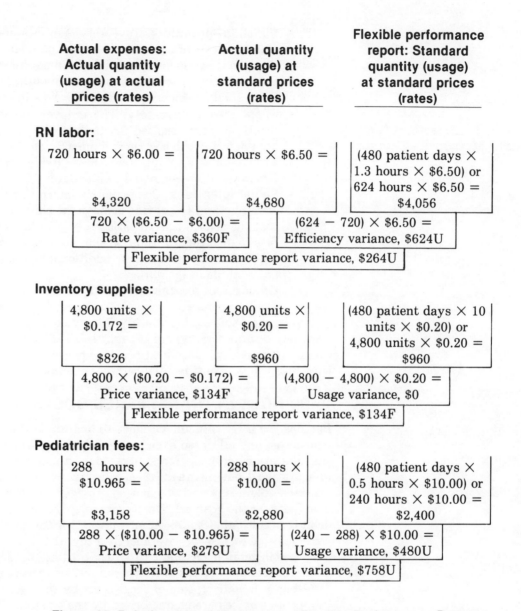

Figure 25. Relationship of Variances to Flexible Performance Report

- **Supplies—inventory.** Inventory supplies usage remained at the standard level of 10 items per patient day. However, two brands were changed that, the purchasing department informs me, are less expensive, resulting in a $135 savings last month. The new items appear to be as good as the previous brands. We will continue to use them.
- **Supplies—noninventory.** The unfavorable variance for noninventoried supplies resulted primarily from purchasing items that had been deferred the last several months; this was a quantity variance. Year-to-date spending on these items, however, still remains favorable when compared to standard.
- **Pediatrician fees.** The pediatric intern, Dr. Kidde, and other staff were required to provide some night shift service during the period that the census was 20 patients. Night shift work is paid at a higher rate than standard, thus causing an unfavorable price variance. The night work, by requiring 48 additional hours, was responsible for the unfavorable usage variance.
- **Other direct expenses.** No explanation for the $25 variance in other direct expenses.

In preparing this variance analysis, any costs that are out of line (either favorably or unfavorably) are brought to the attention of management. Furthermore, individual classifications of expense can be reviewed so that problem areas can be identified and corrective action determined.

VARIANCES IN TRANSFERRED COSTS

Perhaps the most difficult variance to analyze is the variance that concerns transferred and allocated expenses. Analysis is difficult because the transfer and allocation methods for support departments and the general and administrative departments utilize standard rates. These rates are related to the expected volumes of activity in each provider department or the overall level of activity for the hospital. The provider departments will be left with either a debit or credit balance, depending on whether the total cost of those services were underabsorbed or overabsorbed by the user departments. This is described in detail in chapter 8. Also, the provider department will be responsible for providing services at a cost that reflects the long-term level of service resulting in full absorption of those costs by the user.

Support services are characterized by the existence of identifiable units of output that benefit users in proportion to the amount of the service directly consumed. The user department cannot control the costs incurred by the provider department but can control the amount of the service directly consumed (within the limits of hospital policy). The question arises as to whether the user, for the purpose of management control, should be charged with the full cost of the patient care support department service.

If the full cost of the patient care support service is charged to the user, there will be both a price and usage variance for the direct nonlabor expenses. Does the manager of the user department have control over the price variance? The answer is no. At best, the manager of the user department may exert some control indirectly by complaining to administration about the high cost of an hour of housekeeping or of cleaning a pound of laundry. Therefore, the user department manager must control his use of the service as the means of controlling his costs.

This rationale leads to the conclusion that patient care support department services should be charged to user departments at the standard price per service unit. This being the case, departmental performance reports will have only a usage variance for each patient care support department service used. This variance is defined as follows:

Patient care support service usage variance (Q_{PCS})

$$(Q_{PCS}) = \begin{array}{c}\text{Standard price} \\ \text{per unit of} \\ \text{transferred} \\ \text{patient care} \\ \text{support service}\end{array} \times \left[\left(\begin{array}{c}\text{Actual units} \\ \text{of output}\end{array} \times \begin{array}{c}\text{Standard units of} \\ \text{direct patient care} \\ \text{department service} \\ \text{per unit of output}\end{array}\right) - \begin{array}{c}\text{Actual units of} \\ \text{direct patient} \\ \text{department} \\ \text{service used}\end{array}\right]$$

As described in chapter 8, the flexible performance report relationship between direct patient care service department input and user department output might include a fixed as well as a variable component. In those instances, the equation for Q_{PCS} should be divided into a variance in the fixed component and a variance in the variable component. Admittedly, hospital recordkeeping might not provide the necessary detail to perform these computations, nor might it be cost-effective to initiate such recordkeeping. The decision to utilize this degree of detail will be up to individual hospitals after considering various factors, including:

- The degree to which the provider service appears to need more effective control
- The nature of processes involved in providing the service
- The relevant hospital policies governing the service, such as "quality" definitions
- The capital costs required to make operating changes
- The costs of gathering and reporting the information

An example of this can be illustrated using the laundry charges to the pediatric department shown in the sample performance report on page 89. The actual volume of laundry for the pediatrics unit was 12,000 pounds. The standard is computed as follows:

$$\begin{array}{c}\text{The constant of} \\ \text{1,500 pounds} \\ \text{per month}\end{array} + \left(\begin{array}{c}\text{15 pounds per} \\ \text{patient day} \\ \times \text{480 days}\end{array}\right) + \left(\begin{array}{c}\text{30 pounds per} \\ \text{discharge} \times \\ \text{96 discharges}\end{array}\right) = \begin{array}{c}\text{Standard} \\ \text{laundry allowed} \\ \text{for 480 days} \\ \text{and 96} \\ \text{discharges}\end{array}$$

1,500 pounds + 7,200 pounds + 2,880 pounds = 11,580 standard pounds

Therefore, the usage variance is:

$$Q_{PCS} = \$0.25 \times (11{,}580 - 12{,}000) = \$105 \text{ (unfavorable)}$$

This amount represents the variance applicable to both the fixed laundry component and the variance component. A separate variance is not computed in this instance because the fixed and variable portions of actual laundry used are not identifiable. If the fixed/variable variance analysis cannot be performed, the alternative might be to develop only variable flexible budget relationships for the direct patient care department service. These relationships would be proper over a given relevant range of user department output. They should be adjusted, however, for substantial increases or decreases in user department output.

This approach to assigning direct patient care department services to user departments has a reciprocal effect on the provider department. For the provider, the goal will be to attain the standard price per service unit. If this is accomplished, the provider department's expenses will be fully absorbed by the users of the service. The rate variance will, therefore, be provided to the support service department manager.

Patient care support service rate variance (P_{PCS})

$$(P_{PCS}) = \begin{pmatrix} \text{Actual usage of} \\ \text{services of patient} \\ \text{care support} \\ \text{service} \\ \text{department} \end{pmatrix} \times \begin{pmatrix} \text{Standard price} & - & \text{Actual price per} \\ \text{per unit of trans-} & & \text{unit of transferred} \\ \text{ferred patient} & & \text{patient care support} \\ \text{care support} & & \text{service} \\ \text{service} & & \end{pmatrix}$$

Using the laundry department as an example, it was determined through the development of standards that the cost per pound of laundry is 25 cents. If 500,000 pounds of laundry were processed during the month, the users would absorb 500,000 pounds × 25 cents per pound, or \$125,000 of laundry department costs. If actual laundry department costs were \$150,000, laundry service costs would be underabsorbed by the users and the laundry would have an unfavorable flexible budget variance. Similarly, if actual laundry department cost were \$100,000, laundry service costs would be overabsorbed by the users and the laundry would have a favorable flexible budget variance. The interplay, therefore, between the user and provider would then be demonstrated as in figure 26, next page.

This type of interplay emphasizes the major advantage of a cost accounting system with standards. Usage variances are reported to users, who strive to control their use without jeopardizing the quality of service to patients; and rate variances are reported to provider departments, who strive to provide the services required at the optimal level of costs.

The flexible performance report can now be expanded to include variances in transferred costs. This is shown in figure 27, page 104.

VARIANCES IN ALLOCATED COSTS

Overhead services are those provided by the general and administrative departments. These types of services are difficult to identify by units of output that benefit users in proportion to the amount of services provided. Indeed, these overhead services are similar to fixed factory overhead in a manufacturing entity. As such, the extent of expenditures for general and administrative services is related to a measurement of capacity for the hospital.

Hospital management determines a level of expenditure for these services. It is based on a determination of what resources are necessary to support a specific capacity of patient care services. Using this approach, burden rates for general and administrative department services are established by using the standard budget. In the standard budget, the standard costs for each general and administrative service is determined for a standard level of capacity

User: Q_{PCS} favorable Laundry: Underabsorbed	User: Q_{PCS} favorable Laundry: Overabsorbed
Actions Laundry will try to process more pounds to reduce cost per pound to standard price. User will accept until processing more pounds jeopardizes his favorable Q_{PCS}. Result: laundry volume increases thus using more of capacity and reducing unit costs.	**Actions** User is satisfied at current volume. Laundry is efficient in providing user needs. Result: laundry may look for additional service to provide users. Result: potential increase in quality of laundry service.
User: Q_{PCS} unfavorable Laundry: Underabsorbed	User: Q_{PCS} unfavorable Laundry: Overabsorbed
Actions Laundry will try to process more pounds to reduce cost per pound to standard price. User will refuse to have more pounds processed as this increases his unfavorable Q_{PCS}. He will try to reduce pounds processed. Result: laundry must reduce cost to achieve standard price at a potentially lower volume.	**Actions** User will try to reduce pounds of laundry used. Laundry will be able to accommodate decreased volume without decreasing current quality of service. Result: user able to reduce laundry costs.

Figure 26. Sample Laundry Department Budget Variances

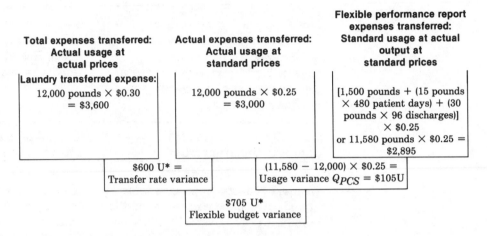

Total expenses transferred: Actual usage at actual prices	Actual expenses transferred: Actual usage at standard prices	Flexible performance report expenses transferred: Standard usage at actual output at standard prices
Laundry transferred expense: 12,000 pounds × $0.30 = $3,600	12,000 pounds × $0.25 = $3,000	[1,500 pounds + (15 pounds × 480 patient days) + (30 pounds × 96 discharges)] × $0.25 or 11,580 pounds × $0.25 = $2,895

$600 U* = Transfer rate variance

$(11,580 - 12,000) \times \$0.25 =$ Usage variance $Q_{PCS} = \$105U$

$705 U* Flexible budget variance

*The transfer rate variances are not the responsibility of the user departments and are not, therefore, shown on the illustrated performance reports in this chapter. They are shown here only to demonstrate the total variance relationships.

Figure 27. Flexible Performance Report with Variances in Transferred Costs

(generally, the projected patient days and outpatient visits for the hospital). From this data, a burden rate can be established on the basis of resource inputs (typically standard labor hours, machine usage, items, and the like) at the standard level of capacity.

For example, assume that the hospital is expected to have 100,000 patient days and 40,000 outpatient visits annually. These facts are used in preparing an annual standard budget to include 1,500,000 standard labor hours. The personnel department is budgeted to require $120,000 at this level of capacity. As a result, the burden rate for the personnel department can be computed as: $120,000 ÷ 1,500,000 standard labor hours = $0.08 per standard labor hour.

Similar computations are made for each general and administrative service. The pediatrics unit was expected to have an average daily census of 18 (540 patient days in a month) in the standard budget, requiring 2,348 standard labor hours. The expected personnel department burden would then be: $0.08 per standard labor hour × 2,348 standard labor hours = $188 of the monthly standard cost of the personnel department. The actual operating results for the month are as follows:

Actual census = 16 (480 patient days)
Actual labor hours = 2,200 hours
Standard labor hours at an average daily census of 16 = 2,114 hours

PERFORMANCE REPORT
Pediatrics unit

Actual personnel department overhead absorbed	Standard overhead absorbed
$0.08 \times 2,200$ hours $= \$176$	$0.08 \times 2,114$ standard hours $= \$169$

There are two usage-type variances in general and administrative service costs. They are as follows:

General and administrative service usage variance (Q_{GA})

$$Q_{GA} = \left[\begin{array}{c} \text{Actual resource} \\ \text{input units at} \\ \text{actual level of} \\ \text{capacity} \end{array} - \left(\begin{array}{c} \text{Actual output} \\ \text{units of service} \end{array} \times \begin{array}{c} \text{Standard resource} \\ \text{input units per} \\ \text{unit of output} \end{array} \right) \right] \times \begin{array}{c} \text{Standard} \\ \text{budget over-} \\ \text{head burden} \\ \text{rate} \end{array}$$

General and administrative service standard budget (volume) variance (V_{GA})

$$V_{GA} = \left[\left(\begin{array}{c} \text{Actual output} \\ \text{units of service} \end{array} \times \begin{array}{c} \text{Standard} \\ \text{resource input} \\ \text{units per unit} \\ \text{of output} \end{array} \right) - \begin{array}{c} \text{Standard budget} \\ \text{input units at} \\ \text{standard budget} \\ \text{level of output} \end{array} \right] \times \begin{array}{c} \text{Standard} \\ \text{budget over-} \\ \text{head burden} \\ \text{rate} \end{array}$$

These calculations can be illustrated using the last example of the personnel department. In this situation, the variances are computed as follows:

Personnel usage variance (Q_{GA})

$$Q_{GA} = \begin{array}{c} \$0.08 \text{ per} \\ \text{labor hour} \end{array} \times \left(\begin{array}{c} 2,200 \text{ actual} \\ \text{labor hours} \end{array} - \left[\begin{array}{c} 242 \text{ fixed} \\ \text{standard} \\ \text{hours} \end{array} + \left(\begin{array}{c} 480 \\ \text{patient} \\ \text{days} \end{array} \times \begin{array}{c} 3.9 \text{ variable} \\ \text{standard} \\ \text{per patient day} \end{array} \right) \right] \right)$$

$$= \$7 \text{ (unfavorable variance)}$$

Personnel volume variance (V_{GA})

$$V_{GA} = \begin{array}{c} \$0.08 \text{ per} \\ \text{labor hour} \end{array} \times \left(\left[\left(\begin{array}{c} 480 \\ \text{patient} \\ \text{days} \end{array} \times \begin{array}{c} 3.9 \text{ standard} \\ \text{hours per} \\ \text{patient day} \end{array} \right) + \begin{array}{c} 242 \text{ fixed} \\ \text{standard} \\ \text{hours} \end{array} \right] - \begin{array}{c} 2,348 \text{ standard} \\ \text{budget labor} \\ \text{hours} \end{array} \right)$$

$$= \$19 \text{ (favorable variance)}$$

For a description of the constant and variable components of the personnel standards used in this example, refer to the example in chapter 9.

In interpreting these results, the usage variance shows the effect of using labor hours in excess of the standard. The standard budget variance, however, denotes the difference in standard overhead applied by achieving 480 patient days rather than the standard budget level of 540. The department's flexible performance reports show only the usage variance, because this is the variance related to management control at the nursing supervisor level.

The computations of the variances for allocated costs can be presented as shown in figure 28, next page, to demonstrate the relationship of the variances to the flexible budget computations. The allocated rate variance is included and calculated in the same way as the rate variance for transferred costs.

In the short term, apart from controlling his own resource utilization, a user department manager cannot control general and administrative overhead usage variances. This initiates the question as to whether a report geared to management control should include applied general and administrative costs. The application of these costs does provide the user department manager with

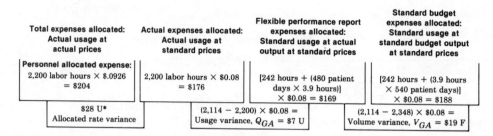

Total expenses allocated: Actual usage at actual prices	Actual expenses allocated: Actual usage at standard prices	Flexible performance report expenses allocated: Standard usage at actual output at standard prices	Standard budget expenses allocated: Standard usage at standard budget output at standard prices
Personnel allocated expense: 2,200 labor hours × $.0926 = $204	2,200 labor hours × $0.08 = $176	[242 hours + (480 patient days × 3.9 hours)] × $0.08 = $169	[242 hours + (3.9 hours × 540 patient days)] × $0.08 = $188
$28 U* Allocated rate variance		(2,114 − 2,200) × $0.08 = Usage variance, Q_{GA} = $7 U	(2,114 − 2,348) × $0.08 = Volume variance, V_{GA} = $19 F

*The allocated rate variances are not the responsibility of the user departments and are not, therefore, shown on the illustrated performance reports in this chapter. They are shown here only to demonstrate the total variance relationships.

Figure 28. Allocated Cost Variances

certain useful information. For example, he can measure the indirect cost to his department of inefficient use of standard units of resources at actual output achieved. Therefore, if general and administrative department service costs are applied to user departments, it does enhance the information available to management for control of costs.

Adding the overhead department costs to the earlier example of the pediatrics unit, the complete flexible performance report is illustrated in table 15, next page.

The variance analysis for direct costs, given earlier in this chapter, applies here as well. In addition, the nursing unit supervisor has information regarding her use of patient care support services and the level of allocation of general and administrative expenses.

PRACTICAL CONSIDERATIONS IN PERFORMING VARIANCE ANALYSIS

As variances are the difference between actual and standard costs, care should be taken in determining the level at which the variance analysis should be performed. To provide the greatest degree of management control, variances should be analyzed for every organized activity or function in the hospital that is performed on a regular basis, can be described by a unit of output, and is directed by a supervisory-level employee. These activities can be routine patient care services, ancillary patient care services, patient care support services, and general and administrative services. Most hospitals perform variance analysis at the cost center level.

For purposes of management control, the closer the defined cost centers represent the aggregation of costs for a homogeneous activity or function, the more precise will be the interpretation of variances from standard. For example, a hospital might use a cost center for the purchasing activity that represents the recording of costs associated with:
- Purchasing inventoriable supplies
- Purchasing noninventoriable supplies and services

Table 15. Complete Monthly Performance Report for a Pediatrics Nursing Floor

	Actual	Standard	Variance	Price/ rate	Usage/ efficiency
Service units:					
Patient days	480				
Average daily census	16				
Patient discharges	96				
Direct expenses:					
Salaries and wages:					
Supervisors	$ 2,500	$ 2,500	$ 0	0	0
RNs	4,320	4,056	264U	360F	$624U
LPNs	3,763	4,080	317F	77F	240F
Nursing assts.	1,680	1,404	276U	120U	156U
Supplies— inventory	825	960	135F	135F	0
Supplies— noninventory	520	300	220U	—	—
Pediatrician fees	3,158	2,400	758U	278U	480U
Other direct expenses	275	250	25U	—	—
Total direct expenses	$17,041	$15,950	$1,091U		
Support expenses (transferred)					
Housekeeping	880	960	80F	—	80F
Laundry	3,000	2,895	105U	—	105U
Maintenance	1,800	1,440	360U	—	360U
Total support expenses	$ 5,680	$ 5,295	$ 385U		
Overhead expenses (allocated)					
Personnel	176	169	7U		7U
Other administrative and general	898	858	40U		40U
Total indirect expenses	1,074	1,027	47U		
Total department expenses	$23,795	$22,272	$1,523U		

- Purchasing capital equipment
- Maintaining the warehouse for inventoriable supplies
- Distributing warehouse and other supplies to consuming departments

No single measure of output is indicative of each of the various activities performed in this cost center. By aggregating labor costs within purchasing, it becomes difficult to isolate the causes of a labor variance.

However, two separate cost centers can be defined for inventoriable supplies (purchasing and handling); and noninventoriable supplies, capital equipment and services (purchasing and handling). As a result, a greater degree of control becomes available through the ability of management to analyze labor variances. For example, for both the inventoriable supplies function and the noninventoriable supplies, equipment and services function, only a single labor variance existed previously.

A hospital could continue this process indefinitely: defining cost centers for noninventoriable supplies, capital equipment purchases, and purchased services separately or defining separate cost centers for the purchasing of inventoriable supplies and the physical handling of inventoriable supplies (the warehousing activity). What limits the extent to which a hospital define functions? There are three factors to consider:

- Ability to account for costs
- Management organization
- Cost effectiveness—the need to know

The ability of the hospital to account for the costs of the defined functions relates directly to the policies and procedures established to properly record expenses at their point of origin. The expenses should then be distributed to the appropriate function, thus incurring the expenses and maintaining sufficient and auditable controls over the process. In the previous example, the accounting system would have to record postage, long distance calls, and supplies expenses incurred by the purchasing cost center in the first situation and by each of the functions (inventory purchasing, warehousing, purchasing noninventoriable supplies, purchasing capital equipment, and purchasing services) in the last situation. It should be clear from this example that the accounting requirements and the cost of maintaining this level of detailed information may indeed limit the fragmenting of functions in this area. In the previous example, if the total annual cost for the function "purchasing outside services" is $1,000 and the marginal cost of separately accounting for this function is $800, there would be nothing to gain unless, through variance analysis, the costs of the "purchasing outside services" function could be reduced by at least $800.

The hospital's management organization can also limit function definition. In the last example, if there is only one supervisor responsible for all noninventory purchases (supplies, equipment, and services), it might be possible for the supervisor to perform the desired variance analysis without incurring the costs of a more detailed functional definition of the area of his responsibility.

DETERMINATION OF APPROPRIATE LEVELS OF ANALYSES

Within the limitations just described, functions may be defined over and above the traditional cost center designations. This is necessary in order to maximize the usefulness of the variance analysis. In the pediatrics unit example of variance analysis, price and usage variances were determined for most of the natural classifications of expense. As in the case of function definition, the question arises as to the cost effectiveness of the analysis of price/usage variances for each natural classification of expense. For example, a $4.53 variance in postage expense is unimportant, but determining the source and cause of a $12,500 efficiency variance in LPN expense is essential. Only a few natural expense classifications make up the vast majority of all expenses in most classification systems in use in hospitals today. It is practical and cost effective to consider how to maximize the use of the payroll system, the purchasing and inventory management system, and the general ledger system. These systems provide the detailed cost information necessary to promote price/usage variance analysis for:

- Labor expenses
- Supplies expenses
- Selected other significant expenses

Labor represents the largest item of expense and provides the largest opportunity for controlling costs. Therefore, significant effort should be placed on the labor variance analysis. In order to facilitate a labor variance analysis, labor hours and expenses should be recorded by personnel classification within each cost center (function) used for cost identification. Care should be taken when choosing appropriate personnel classification to promote effective variance analysis.

As described in chapter 5, supplies can be subclassified into many categories. In the extreme, each item of supply is identified. This process is accomplished for inventoriable supplies by use of an inventory management system. Using an inventory stock numbering system, each item of supply used can be accounted for within the inventory system. Standards can be established for use of stock items by each cost center and for item prices. The key to identifying actual supplies costs is in the accounting for these costs by functional activity. Appropriate requisitioning procedures should be implemented to provide control over this process.

Generally, noninventory supplies do not lend themselves to price/usage variance analysis. In most instances, these items are not consumed in relation to output, nor are they well defined prior to their actual purchase. At best, for this expense, the total flexible performance report variance can be analyzed for increases or decreases in the actual level of expenditures.

The cost effectiveness of developing standard price and usage variables for each remaining expense classification should be examined before accepting a single flexible budget variance for them all. Expenses such as employee benefits, professional fees, telephone, and utilities can be subject to potentially beneficial price/usage variance analyses.

SPECIAL ANALYSES IN TRANSFERRED AND ALLOCATED COSTS

In the pediatrics unit illustration, the treatment of overhead expenses incurred and the interpretation of variances were discussed. The major consideration in transferring patient care support department expenses to user departments is the service unit defined for each activity. A homogeneous service unit for one hospital's management may be unacceptable for another. For example, the dietary department may have patient meals as the service unit. A more precise service unit would be type of patient meal. The following example illustrates the potential benefit in using the more precise service unit.

Given
Standard price per patient meal — $2.00
Pediatrics standard meals per patient days — 3.00
Pediatrics actual patient days — 480
Pediatrics standard meals per actual patient days — 1,440
Pediatrics actual meals ordered — 1,540

Pediatrics department variance analysis

	Actual	Standard	Variance
Dietary expense	$3,080	$2,880	$200U

A review of the dietary department's standards for pediatrics reveals the following information:

Standard cost per meal

	Breakfast	Lunch	Dinner	Snacks
Regular diet	$1.00	$2.00	$3.00	$1.70
Salt-free diet	1.50	2.50	3.50	2.55
Liquid-only diet	.75	1.50	2.25	.85
Hi-protein diet	1.25	2.25	3.25	1.00
No-fat diet	1.25	2.25	3.25	1.00

It can be seen that, although the overall standard price per meal is $2.00, the variance for pediatrics can be significantly improved by further analysis.

Given
Pediatrics standard usage

	Breakfast	Lunch	Dinner	Snacks	Total
Regular diet	0.60	0.30	0.60	0.40	1.90
Salt-free diet	0.15	0.05	0.15	0.05	0.40
Liquid-only diet	0.05	0.05	0.05	0.05	0.20
Hi-protein diet	0.10	0.05	0.10		0.25
No-fat diet	0.10	0.05	0.10		0.25
Total	1.00	0.50	1.00	0.50	3.00

Pediatrics actual meals ordered

	Breakfast	Lunch	Dinner	Snacks	Total
Regular diet	253	177	250	167	847
Salt-free diet	113	51	108	36	308
Liquid-only diet	26	43	30	30	129
Hi-protein diet	44	34	46	4	128
No-fat diet	44	35	46	3	128
Total	480	340	480	240	1,540

Pediatrics standard cost of actual meals

	Breakfast	Lunch	Dinner	Snacks	Total
Regular diet	$253.00	$354.00	$ 750.00	$283.90	$1,640.00
Salt-free diet	169.50	127.50	378.00	91.80	766.80
Liquid-only diet	19.50	64.50	67.50	25.50	177.00
Hi-protein diet	55.00	76.50	149.50	4.00	285.00
No-fat diet	55.00	78.75	149.50	3.00	286.25
Total	$552.00	$701.25	$1,494.50	$408.20	$3,155.05

Pediatrics department variance analysis

	Actual	Standard	Variance
Volume (meals)	1,540	1,440	100
Dietary department	$3,080	$2,880	$200U

An analysis of these results indicates that the variance was the result of a significant increase in lunches ordered and in salt-free diet meals ordered compared to standard usage. This is a significantly more detailed analysis than one that is performed using patient meals as the service unit. Hospital management is again faced with the cost/benefit issue. It may be appropriate to use the homogeneous standard on a day-to-day basis and undertake a more detailed analysis or special study if variances persist.

Finally, when implementing a cost accounting system, care should be taken in establishing allocation bases for overhead. The most meaningful allocations use a basis that reflects the benefits provided by the service. Some allocation units might be:

- Personnel—labor hours
- Admitting—admissions by admitting locations (weighted and pro-rated, if necessary)
- Printing—job order (labor or cost)

One benefit from using a standard cost system is the ability, through the process of setting standards, to develop application bases that more directly reflect general and administrative services.

CHAPTER 11

Key Issues in Implementation

The successful implementation of a cost accounting system includes accurate measurement of both the expenditure of resources and the results of management's efforts to control costs. As stated earlier, a flexible budget is a hospital's quantified operational plan. Through the use of standards, flexible performance reports, and the calculation of variances, management can measure its success in achieving its financial plan despite the fact that the utilization of the hospital's services might be different from the levels proposed in the budget. Management can couple this information with reports that address the quality of services provided, employee morale, the interests of the medical staff, and the needs of the community. As a result, management can then choose to commit resources to the most appropriate functions in order to maintain the levels of quality and service provided by the institution. A cost accounting system will also provide management with the information necessary to identify departments that require corrective action and will highlight areas that could benefit from modifications in methods and procedures.

The maximum benefit can be derived from the system if the hospital carries on the following activities:

- Maintenance of the credibility of the standards
- Preparation and use of timely and accurate flexible performance reports
- Development and implementation of a responsibility reporting system

The remainder of this chapter deals with these activities and their role in effectively using a cost accounting system.

MAINTENANCE OF THE CREDIBILITY OF STANDARDS

A cost accounting system compares actual performance with standard performance. The standards used should represent achievable levels of effort for hospital personnel, not ideal or projected levels. This requires:

- Monitoring services provided in a statistical data gathering and reporting system
- Periodic revision of standards to reflect substantial changes in methods and procedures
- Costing standards at rates or prices indicative of the current operating environment

This process will use personnel, supplies, and services above current levels. These additional resources should be cost effective, however, as managers create offsetting cost savings as a result of the additional information provided by the system.

A cost accounting staff should be established to maintain accurate standards, assist in methods improvement, and perform special studies for strategic planning. A sample standards maintenance checklist is illustrated in figure 29, next page. The cost accounting staff should consist primarily of cost

Task	Date completed	By
A. Review		
1. Review standard methods and procedures		
2. Review workpapers for previous studies		
3. Review standards notification file		
B. Plan		
1. Summarize previous work performed		
2. Prepare work program and schedule of maintenance activities		
3. Work program approved		
C. Perform		
1. Complete familiarization work		
2. Prepare worksheets for studies		
3. Perform studies		
4. Tabulate results		
D. Document		
1. Prepare rate/price change requests		
2. Prepare standards change requests		
3. Prepare workload data change requests		
4. Prepare employee time collection records request		
5. Prepare personnel classification/shift updates		
6. Sign off standards maintenance change requests		
7. Requests approved		
E. Update		
1. Standard cost accounting manuals		
2. Methods improvement list for future action		
F. Report		
1. Prepare summary of work performed		
2. Prepare report to department manager		
G. Final review		
1. Final review of maintenance work		
2. Maintenance work completed and approved		

Figure 29. Standards Maintenance Program Checklist

accountants and management engineers. The exact number of staff will vary with the size of the hospital, the level of sophistication of the system, and the complexity of the management organization.

There are significant benefits to the establishment of accurate, achievable standards. Managers are less likely to explain variances by stating that standards are inaccurate. They can then focus on the real sources and causes of variances. When analyzing methods and procedures, staff will find improved ways to perform old functions. These new methods will extend the hospital's resources and will reduce unfavorable variances or improve favorable variances. In special studies, cost accounting system data can be used to determine the impact of decisions affecting capacity, service mix, and other strategic factors in the hospital. With credible standards in place, the next step in implementing the system is the preparation of flexible performance reports.

PREPARATION OF FLEXIBLE PERFORMANCE REPORTS

Flexible performance reports, addressed in chapter 9, are an essential element of the cost accounting system. These reports should be timely and accurate. However, the achievement of one such report sometimes means a sacrifice in the other.

Performance reports should be available immediately following the relevant time period for the activity reported. In so doing, the report will be less accurate (in an accounting sense). However, a loss in accuracy should be sacrificed for prompt report generation if it does not materially distort the cost accounting process. Management can take many actions to ensure that the loss in accuracy is minimal.

Delayed performance reports are of limited use for management control. When preparing performance reports, management can choose to provide daily, weekly, biweekly, monthly, quarterly, annual, or other reports. The frequency of reporting will depend on the nature of the activity being measured and the cost implications of allowing significant variances to go unreported. For example, a nursing unit might require weekly reports, while the vice-president for nursing might need only quarterly reports. Generally speaking, the higher in the organization a manager is situated, the more fixed are the short-run costs of the functions over which he is responsible. The reports generated should reflect this.

With the increasing use of modern data collection equipment, computers, and information systems, the incidence of delayed performance reports will diminish.

The key to accuracy in flexible performance reports is an increased level of discipline over input data required for the various accounting systems. Management should encourage and enforce a high level of discipline for the recording of financial and operating transactions. Several areas that require special attention are employee time reporting, payroll expenses, nonlabor expenses, and statistical data. The following is a discussion of these areas.

Time Reporting   Time reporting is a minimal activity that does not interfere with an employee's job. A cost accounting system requires more specific time reporting so that labor performance measurements can be calculated. Time should be assigned to a financial accounting system cost center. In addition, employees should record time in many categories:

- Time spent on predetermined functions within an assigned cost center or other cost center
- Hours worked on various shifts
- Time spent on authorized absences (vacation, holiday, sick leave, and the like)
- Time spent working in different pay categories or in different personnel classifications
- Overtime hours spent on predetermined functions
- Total hours worked for salaried personnel with a breakdown as described in the preceding points

Time recording requires that employees both understand the need for detailed information and participate by recording their efforts. Furthermore, management will have to review employee time reports and take responsibility for the data submitted. The imposition of these requirements on hospital employees can cause resentment. Therefore, it is extremely important that management monitor this activity closely, alleviate employee fears, and convey the importance of timekeeping to each employee. The ability of the flexible performance system to accurately report labor efficiency is predicated on detailed, accurate labor utilization data.

Payroll Expenses

The payroll system must be capable of translating detailed time records into appropriately identified costs. Most payroll systems can be modified to provide this information accurately. However, there are several policy decisions that must be addressed by management to obtain proper costing of personnel services. For example:

- Function costing of paid absences
- Timing of accruals
- Nonpayroll-related fringe benefits

The first of these areas is concerned with identifying the function to be charged with the cost of vacation, holidays, sick leave, and other paid absences that accrue during the normal operating cycle. The cost accounting process requires the matching of these costs with functions regularly performed by each employee in proportion to his productive efforts. This rationale is closest to the method used for establishing labor standards for each function performed and, as such, will provide the most consistent data for variance analysis.

The second area requiring policy determination is the timing of accruals. The need for accruals results from a time lag between the incurrence of a cost and the payment of that cost. Two cases requiring accruals are vacation pay and pension plan contribution. In addition to establishing the items falling into this category, the appropriate accrual rates must be determined. The usual procedure of setting standards is to determine a standard burden rate for each item and add it to the standard labor rate. This has the effect of averaging these expenses throughout the year.

However, many of these expenses occur at rates other than the annual average rate. For example, Federal Insurance Contribution Act (FICA) tax is accrued at a specified rate on wages earned up to a statutory maximum. As the year progresses, more employees pass the maximum, and the expense decreases. Is it fair to load these costs in the early part of the year? The answer might lie in assessing the costs of maintaining more accurate accruals in comparison with the information enhancement obtained.

These same issues apply to the third area, nonpayroll-related fringe benefits. Items such as life and health insurance premiums should be identified with productive labor. Management should recognize the variances caused by payroll costing techniques and not penalize front line supervisors for the resultant deviations from plan.

Nonlabor Expenses

The recording of nonlabor expenses is dependent upon a number of source documents, including:

- Purchase orders
- Inventory requisitions
- Invoices
- Check requests
- Contracts
- Vouchers
- Phone logs
- Postage meters
- Utility meter readings
- Insurance agreements
- Journal entry forms

In order to support cost identification, source documents must include quantity, unit price, extended price (including discounts), account distribution to the appropriate function, and classification of expense.

Policies and procedures can be established to delay approval for these expenditures until the proper data is obtained. This action may generate some resistance from employees but must be performed to achieve function-level performance reporting. Recording of nonlabor expenses at their origination will increase their accuracy, consistency, and credibility in flexible performance reports.

Output Volume Data

The maintenance of statistical records and reports is as important as the recording of properly identified costs. Standard resource usage and costs are determined with computations involving output volume. As such, performance reports require output data to be readily available. The recording, compiling, and summarizing of these data should be performed with the frequency necessary to prepare flexible performance reports. There are several actions that management can perform to facilitate statistical data collection:

- Establish a classification system for volume statistics that permits direct correlation to the standard with which they are used.
- Require units of output to be recorded in this classification system when they are "produced." This will allow reports to be produced at variable intervals by using output volume to date.
- Establish periodic audit procedures to control the statistical data collection process. The audit activity could be performed by the cost accounting staff. It would ensure that it is recorded when produced and that data are properly counted and classified according to the definition of the unit of data.

Historically, hospitals have had difficulty using standard costs. This was largely a result of errors in the determination of statistical data. Through the cost accountng system, volume data are a distinct part of the financial reporting and management control system of the hospital. Collecting volume data is a part of the management control process. Such data are beneficial to management through the increased accuracy and usefulness of flexible performance reports.

In summary, it is imperative that timely and accurate flexible performance reports are produced to effectively use the cost accounting system. Although some accuracy may be lost for promptness, it will not detract from the usefulness of the reports for management control. Revisions to achieve accounting accuracy can be performed at a later date, and the revised report filed for future reference.

DEVELOPMENT AND IMPLEMENTATION OF RESPONSIBILITY REPORTING SYSTEM

The purpose of responsibility reporting is to identify resources that deviate from plan for the individual who can take action through direct control over those resources. A responsibility reporting system is a system in which flexible performance reports are prepared that reflect the hospital's management hierarchy. They must include the appropriate detail for maximum use by each management level.

Figure 22, page 85, depicts a typical responsibility reporting system. In this system, reports are prepared in great detail at the function level (chemistry laboratory), in lesser detail at the cost center level (clinical laboratories), summarized at the department level (pathology department), and further summarized at the administrative level (professional services) and in the hospital-wide report.

When the responsibility reporting system is combined with cost accounting and variance analysis, the essential informational elements for cost management are in place. Using these elements to achieve optimal use of resources requires management to motivate employees to work within the system toward this goal. Whether encouragement is accomplished by wage incentives, promotion, or other personal acknowledgements is an individual matter. However, management cannot ignore positive reinforcement if the benefits of management control are to be achieved.

As stated earlier, performance reports should be generated at differing intervals to reflect managers' requirements for cost information. For example, the chemistry laboratory section chief has a greater degree of control over next week's staffing and supplies than does the director of the pathology department. However, the latter certainly has more control over the level of expenditures in the chemistry laboratory in the future, through consideration of hospital census, patient mix, capital equipment purchases, and methods and procedures changes (such as computerized order entry and results reporting). The two working together with a clear sense of costs and output can maximize the use of the system.

The responsibility reporting system is a dynamic process of interaction between and among management and employees. The system operates in the following generalized manner:

Step 1. Output for each relevant time period is applied to the standards for each activity to produce a standard cost and usage at actual output.

Step 2. Standard cost and usage at actual output is compared to actual cost and usage for each time period in performance reports. These reports reveal variances in the use of resources for the actual output achieved.

Step 3. The variances revealed by the reports are analyzed by management to determine their causes. The analyses are made at the appropriate level of detail or in summary, as appropriate.

Step 4. Corrective actions are discussed between superior and subordinate at each organization level. From this, a plan is developed to correct the causes of the variances with the goal of bringing resource utilization to optimal (or acceptable) levels. These actions may result from front line managerial decisions, through collective decisions of responsible individuals at several managerial levels, or through recommendations based on the findings of special studies performed by the cost accounting staff.

Step 5. The plan of corrective action is implemented by managers with written procedures and employee training.

Step 6. The plan is monitored in subsequent flexible performance reports, interim reports, and variance analysis.

Step 7. The plan of action is modified or a new plan prepared on the basis of subsequent performance against standard.

The process, as described here, is repeated on a regular basis in response to the variances reported. The result is an effective process to promote operational effectiveness with performance measures, stated objectives, and an information system. As with any management system, proper employee motivation is the most essential prerequisite to achieve the desired results. Success is dependent upon management taking a positive approach in implementing the cost accounting and responsibility reporting systems.

The proper approach should include some of the following organizational factors:

- Visible support by hospital administration
- Active support at all managerial levels
- Presentation of goals and objectives of the system to all employees
- Clear description of each employee's role in the success of the system
- Description of the performance evaluation process related to using the system including potential rewards and discipline
- Written procedures governing the operational requirements of the system (who, what, where, when, why, and how)

In summary, the elements of cost accounting, performance reporting, and variance analysis combine to provide an effective system for management control. In order to achieve the maximum results from the system, management should recognize three critical requirements:

- Maintaining credibility of the standards
- Ensuring the timeliness and accuracy of the flexible performance reports
- Implementing a responsibility reporting system

These elements provide an environment in which the data obtained through the cost accounting process can be combined with other management information to promote the optimal use of hospital resources in providing high-quality services to its patients.

Absorption costing. The process of allocating (full absorption costing) or apportioning (direct and standard costing) fixed and variable production costs to work in process, cost of sales, and inventory. See also *marginal costing.*

Allocated cost. The apportionment of expenses incurred by indirect cost centers that remain undistributed after direct transfers.

Contribution margin or *marginal income.* The excess of gross revenue over related direct cost.

Cost accounting system. A hybrid system combining features of both process and job order cost systems.

Cost finding. The apportionment or allocation of the costs of nonrevenue-producing cost centers to each other and to revenue-producing cost centers on the basis of the statistical data that measure the amount of service rendered by each center to other centers.

Cost information system. A system that accounts for cost by responsibility center and generates basic management performance reports.

Diagnostic-related group. A means of classifying patients into groups that are homogeneous in terms of reasons for hospitalization and the treatment regimen provided.

Indirect overhead. Cost that cannot be identified with specific services rendered by patient care departments or patient support departments and that therefore is allocated on some reasonable basis.

Marginal costing. The assignment of only marginal or variable costs to an activity or department as contrasted with full absorption costing. Marginal costing deals only with incremental costs, whereas absorption costing relates to average cost. See also *absorption costing.*

Mixed cost. A cost that has both fixed and variable components.

Natural expense classification or *object classification.* The original designation of an acquired good or service pending its functional spread.

Overhead. Any cost of doing business other than a direct cost of an output of service.

Relevant range. The band of activity in which the relationship between budgeted charges and expenses will be valid.

Transferred cost. The passage of the costs of goods and supplies from the inventory holding or central stores department to the user departments for further consumption.

Index